Internet Research
Illustrated

Donald I. Barker
Robert Schroeder

THOMSON
★
COURSE TECHNOLOGY

Australia • Canada • Mexico • Singapore • Spain • United Kingdom • United States

THOMSON

COURSE TECHNOLOGY

Internet Research - Illustrated

Donald I. Barker, Robert Schroeder

Managing Editor:
Nicole Jones Pinard

Senior Product Manager:
Emily Heberlein

Associate Product Manager:
Christina Kling Garrett

Production Editor:
Anne Valsangiacomo

Developmental Editor:
Jane Hosie-Bounar

Editorial Assistant:
Elizabeth M. Harris

QA Manuscript Reviewers:
Jeff Schwartz, Nick Atlas

Text Designer:
Joseph Lee, Black Fish Design

Composition House:
GEX Publishing Services

The Illustrated Series Vision

Teaching and writing about computer applications and information literacy can be extremely rewarding and challenging. How do we engage students and keep their interest? How do we teach them skills that they can easily apply on the job? As we set out to write this book, our goals were to develop a textbook that:

- ▶ works for a beginning student
- ▶ provides varied, flexible and meaningful exercises and projects to reinforce the skills
- ▶ serves as a reference tool
- ▶ makes your job as an educator easier, by providing resources above and beyond the textbook to help you teach your course

Our popular, streamlined format is based on advice from instructional designers and customers. This flexible design presents each lesson on a two-page spread, with step-by-step instructions on the left, and screen illustrations on the right. This signature style, coupled with high-caliber content, provides a comprehensive introduction to the crucial skills of conducting Internet research — it is a teaching package for the instructor and a learning experience for the student.

ACKNOWLEDGMENTS

Creating a book is a team effort: We would like to thank our wives, Chia-Ling and Laura, for their patience, understanding, and support, Nicole Pinard, for publishing the book, Emily Heberlein, for managing the project, and our development editor, Jane Hosie-Bounar, for her suggestions and corrections. Special thanks to the production, editorial, and marketing staff for all their hard work. Finally, we are very grateful to Jerry Tardif of Bright Planet for providing a semester-length trial version of LexiBot.

Donald I. Barker and Robert Schroeder
Spokane Falls Community College

Preface

Welcome to *Internet Research–Illustrated*. Each lesson in the book contains elements pictured to the right in the sample two-page spread.

► How is the book organized?

The book is organized into four units on conducting effective Internet research, from conducting basic searches with search engines using keywords and phrases, to creating complex searches using Boolean logic. Subject guides and specialized tools are also covered, including periodical databases, government resources, online reference sources, and mailing lists and newsgroups.

► What kinds of assignments are included in the book? At what level of difficulty?

The lesson assignments use the interesting and relevant case study of alternative energy. As part of the city planning office in Portland, Oregon, you conduct research in order to establish policies for the city to become "energy independent." The assignments on the blue pages at the end of each unit increase in difficulty. Assignments include:

• **Concepts Reviews** include multiple choice, matching, and screen identification questions.

• **Skills Reviews** provide additional hands-on, step-by-step reinforcement.

• **Independent Challenges** are case projects requiring critical thinking and application of the skills learned in the unit. The Independent Challenges increase in difficulty, with the first Independent Challenge in each unit being the easiest (most step-by-step with detailed instructions). Further Independent Challenges become increasingly open-ended, requiring more independent thinking and problem solving.

• **Visual Workshops** show a completed file or Web page and require that the file be created or accessed without any step-by-step guidance, involving problem solving and an independent application of the unit skills.

Each 2-page spread focuses on a single skill.

Concise text introduces the basic principles in the lesson and integrates the brief case study (indicated by the paintbrush icon).

B Internet Research

Searching with Filters

Another great way to refine and focus a search is by using filters. Filters are programs that search engines use to screen out Web pages and other files on the World Wide Web. They are usually located at a search engine's Advanced Search page. Before you type your search query, you can choose filters to block out large areas of the Web from your search. For example, you can use language filters to search only for Web pages written in English, or you can use date filters to search only for Web pages updated in the last year. Filters are often activated by choosing from a pull-down menu or by typing special filter command words in the Search text box, examples of which are shown in Table B-4. Different Web file types like images, audio, or video can also be filter choices at search engines. ✎ A colleague in your office told you that Denmark is a leader in wind power. You want to locate wind power sites from Denmark, but since your Danish is a bit rusty you need to find only Web pages in English. You will use filters to focus your search.

Steps

QuickTip
In the URL, notice the underline between the words *advanced* and *search*. There are never any spaces in URLs. Often what appear to be spaces are underlines or hyphens.

QuickTip
Notice that the Domains filter lets you choose between "*Only* return results from the site or domain" or "*Don't* return results from the site or domain."

QuickTip
Google also has a great Image Search with an advanced Image Search page that uses filters. Filters unique to Image Searching include size (from icon to wallpaper); file types (GIF, JPG); and coloration (from black and white to full color).

1. Go to the Student Online Companion at **www.course.com/illustrated/research**, click the **Google Search** link, then click **Advanced Search** (to the right of the Search text box)
The Google Advanced Search page appears.

2. Click the **Language** filter pull-down menu, then choose **English**
English should be selected, as in Figure B-19. Using this filter, you will only find Web pages written in English. Now you want to restrict your search to the domain exclusive to Denmark, which appears as *dk* in the URL.

3. Type **.dk** in the Domains filter text box
The Domains text box should appear as in Figure B-19. Using this filter you will only find Web pages in Denmark. (For more on Domains, see "The parts of a URL" Clues box.)

4. Type **wind power** in the Exact phrase text box, then click the **Google Search button**
Your search results should resemble those shown in Figure B-23. The Web pages in the set of results should contain the phrase *wind power*, should be written in English, and should be located in the Denmark domain.

5. Use the Project File to record some of the things you notice about the Search results page
For example, look in the Search text box on your results page, or at Figure B-20. Google has translated your search as "*wind power*" site:.dk. The *site:.dk* is how Google translated your choice of .dk in the Domains filter. Look also just below the tabs at the top left of the search results page. Google reiterated your search query as Searched *English* pages for "*wind power*" *site:.dk*. This information provides a good way to determine whether the filters worked the way you thought they would when you set up your search.

6. Save, print, and close the Project File

TABLE B-4: **Examples of filters available at Google**

Text box or pull-down menu filters	**Language** limits your search to sites written in the language you choose. **Date** limits your search to Web pages updated within a specified time period. **Domains** limits your search to words found at a certain domain name or type (.edu, .com, etc.). **SafeSearch** limits your search to child-friendly sites.
Command word filters (used in the regular search text box)	**inurl** limits your search to words found directly in the URL. **intitle** limits your search to words found in the title of a Web page. **site** limits your search to words found at a certain domain name or type (.edu, .com, etc.). **link** finds only Web pages linked to a specified URL.

► INTERNET RESEARCH B-14 **CONSTRUCTING DEEP SEARCHES**

Hints, as well as troubleshooting advice, right where you need them — next to the step itself.

Quickly accessible summaries of key terms and strategies connected with the lesson material. You can refer easily to this information when working on your own projects at a later time.

Every lesson features large, full-color representations of conceptual art or of what the screen should look like as you complete the numbered steps.

FIGURE B-19: Google filtered search set-up

Boolean and search
Boolean phrase search
Boolean or search
Boolean and not search
Filters

Exact phrase text box
Language filter pull-down menu
Domains filter text box

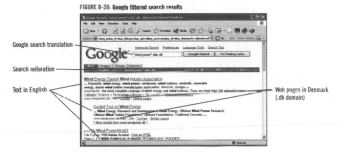

FIGURE B-20: Google filtered search results

Google search translation
Search reiteration
Text in English

Web pages in Denmark (.dk domain)

CLUES TO USE

The parts of a URL

Filters, such as Domains and site, search only for words that appear in parts of a URL. The URL www.wind.dk/english/home/html, for example, has the following parts:
www.wind.dk /english /home .html
domain *file* *page* *file extension*
For Web sites in the United States, the last part of a domain name can be three letters that represent the type of organization hosting the Web site. University

domains often end in .edu; government sites end in .gov; commercial sites end in .com; and non-profits end in .org. Web sites located in other countries use two-letter country codes, like .fr for France, .uk for the United Kingdom, and .de for Germany (Deutschland). Any of these two- or three-letter codes can be used to limit search results when using filters. For a full listing of the two-letter country codes, go to www.iana.org/cctld/cctld-whois.htm.

Internet Research

Clues to Use boxes provide concise information that either expands on the major lesson skill or describes an independent task that in some way relates to the major lesson skill.

► What Web resources supplement the book?

The Illustrated Series has partnered with BrightPlanet to bring you a trial version of LexiBot, an intelligent search agent, used in Unit D. LexiBot is available for download from www.course.com/illustrated/research/download.html. See the Read This Before You Begin page for further instructions and information on LexiBot.

Internet Research–Illustrated also features a Student Online Companion (SOC) Web site. Use the SOC to access all the links referenced in the book, and to access other resources for further information. Since the Internet and search engines change frequently, the SOC will also contain any updates or clarifications to the text after its publication.

► What online learning options are available to accompany this book?

Options for this title include a testbank in MyCourse 2.0, WebCT and Blackboard ready formats to make assessment using one of these platforms easy to manage. Visit www.course.com for more information on our online learning materials.

Instructor Resources

The Instructor's Resource Kit (IRK) CD is Course Technology's way of putting the resources and information needed to teach and learn effectively into your hands. All the components are available on the IRK CD, and many of the resources can be downloaded from www.course.com.

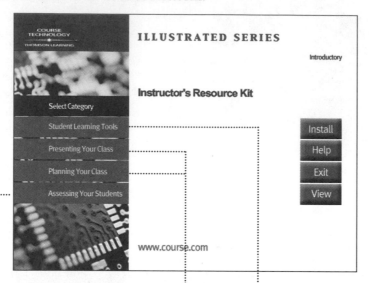

ASSESSING YOUR STUDENTS

Solution Files
Solution Files are Project Files completed with comprehensive sample answers. Use these files to evaluate your students' work. Or, distribute them electronically or in hard copy so students can verify their own work.

ExamView
ExamView is a powerful testing software package that allows you to create and administer printed, computer (LAN-based), and Internet exams. ExamView includes hundreds of questions that correspond to the topics covered in this text, enabling students to generate detailed study guides that include page references for further review. The computer-based and Internet testing components allow students to take exams at their computers, and also save you time by grading each exam automatically.

PRESENTING YOUR CLASS

Figure Files
Figure Files contain all the figures from the book in bmp format. Use the figure files to create transparency masters or in a PowerPoint presentation.

STUDENT TOOLS

Project Files and Project Files List
To complete the units in this book, your students will need **Project Files**. Put them on a file server for students to copy. The Project Files are available on the Instructor's Resource Kit CD-ROM, the Review Pack, and can also be downloaded from www.course.com.

Instruct students to use the **Project Files List** at the end of the book. This list gives instructions on copying and organizing files.

PLANNING YOUR CLASS

Instructor's Manual
Available as an electronic file, the Instructor's Manual is quality-assurance tested and includes unit overviews, detailed lecture topics for each unit with teaching tips, comprehensive sample solutions to all lessons and end-of-unit material, and extra Independent Challenges. The Instructor's Manual is available on the Instructor's Resource Kit CD-ROM, or you can download it from www.course.com.

Sample Syllabus
Prepare and customize your course easily using this sample course outline (available on the Instructor's Resource Kit CD-ROM).

Contents

⌐ Internet Research ⌐

Read This Before You Begin

Are there any prerequisites for this book?

This book focuses on using the Internet effectively as a powerful research tool. It assumes that you are familiar with the Internet and Internet terms, and know basic Web-browsing skills. Basic Web-browsing skills include using the menus and toolbars in the browser of your choice, entering URLs, and navigating the Web using hyperlinks. In order to complete the exercises using the Project Files, you should also have basic word-processing skills.

What software do I need in order to use this book?

You will need an Internet connection, a Web browser and a text-editing or word-processing program, such as Microsoft Word or WordPad, in order to complete the lessons and exercises in this book. You can be running any recent version of the Windows operating system after and including Windows 95, and can also use the Mac operating system for every lesson but the last lesson in the book. (This lesson uses LexiBot. See below for more information). This book was written and tested using Microsoft Internet Explorer 6 and Microsoft Windows XP. If you are working with a different browser or in a different operating system, your screens might look slightly different than those shown in the book. However, your results should be similar. In addition, all the steps and exercises have been tested using Netscape 4.7 with Windows 98 and Netscape 6.2 with Windows 2000. The Project Files have been verified in these environments and on Mac OS 10 as well.

In order to complete the last lesson in Unit D, "Searching with Intelligent Agents," and to complete Skills Review 8 and Independent Challenge 4 in Unit D, you need to download and install **LexiBot**, an Internet search tool that allows you to simultaneously search 150 of a possible 2200 search sources. If you are taking the class in a lab, and your instructor is covering this topic, your instructor or lab administrator will take care of the installation for you. If you are working through the steps on your own computer, you can download LexiBot from www.course.com/illustrated/research/download.html. This software is an educational trial version. After installing this special release of LexiBot, you will have 126 days to use it before it expires. If you are working from a dial-up Internet connection, advanced searches using LexiBot will take a while to complete. A fast Internet connection is recommended. Please see the download page and Frequently Asked Questions for further information. For instructors and lab administrators who will need access to LexiBot for more than one semester, please see the Instructor's Manual for instructions on extending the trial version time.

What are Project Files and how do I use them?

Project Files are text files in rich-text format that you use to answer questions about your research results. You use a Project File in most lessons and in some of the exercises. Typically, you open the designated file and save it with a new name.

What is the Student Online Companion and how do I use it?

You use the Student Online Companion (SOC), located at www.course.com/illustrated/research, to access all the links used in the book. Because the Internet and its search engines change frequently, the SOC will provide updates to the text as necessary. To access the SOC quickly, add the SOC URL to your Favorites or Bookmarks, or set it as your home page. (If you are working in a lab, please ask your instructor before doing this.) The URL is provided throughout the book in steps and tips for easy reference as well.

Unit A

Searching
the Internet Effectively

Objectives

► **Understand the Internet, the Web, and search engines**
► **Create an Internet research strategy**
► **Find the right keywords**
► **Perform a basic search**
► **Morph keywords and use wildcards**
► **Use phrases**
► **Metasearch**
► **Cite online resources**

The World Wide Web is a huge repository of information stored on hundreds of thousands of computers all over the world. The Internet is a vast network that allows you to connect to all of the Web's information. Finding information can seem deceptively easy. In fact, finding lots of information is often easier than finding the right information. In this unit you will learn about the Internet, the Web, and the nature of Internet search engines. You will also learn how to transform your initial question into a **search query** designed to locate the information you seek on the Web. ▬▬▬ You work in Portland, Oregon's City Planning Office. The citizens have recently passed a proposition that mandates that Portland become "energy independent" in the near future. You are working with a team to create a Web resource for city officials and citizens. You have been charged with using the Internet to locate Web pages related to potential alternative energy sources.

Internet Research

Understanding the Internet, the Web, and Search Engines

The Internet is vast and ever-changing, and along with the World Wide Web, it has streamlined research, putting thousands of resources literally at your fingertips. Internet **search engines** are search tools that can help you locate information on the Internet. As with all tools, understanding how they work and how to use them effectively will improve your results. ✎ Before you start your search for Web pages about alternative energy sources, you decide to learn more about the Internet, the Web, and Internet search engines by studying the following information.

Internet and World Wide Web basics:

► The **Internet** is an enormous network of networks that share a common communication standard. It enables computers all over the world to exchange information.

► The **World Wide Web** (WWW), or the Web, is a vast collection of documents and other media linked together over the Internet. **Web pages** are the most common type of document. Web pages are usually written in hypertext markup language (html for short) with file extensions of .htm or .html. They can include text, links to other pages, and links to images, audio, or video clips. Over 1 billion Web pages currently exist, and about 1 million pages are added each day.

► You can access these web pages at a **Web site**. A Web site can range in size from one Web page to thousands of Web pages. There are over 5 million Web sites on the Internet.

► Information exists on the Web in many other formats, too. For example, pictures and images are stored in **GIF** or **JPG** format. Audio files for music are in **MP3** format, and video files for movies are in **MOV** format. Table A-1 lists other file formats and their extensions.

► Not only can you view material that others have created on the Web, you can interact with others using e-mail and newsgroups. Having an e-mail account also lets you join mailing lists comprised of people who share your interest in a particular topic or topics. You can use a mailing list to communicate via e-mail with hundreds (or thousands) of people at once.

Search engine basics:

QuickTip

To find out more about search engines, click the Search Engine Watch or Search Engine Showdown link in the Student Online Companion, at www.course.com/illustrated/research.

► A **search engine** is a special kind of Web site that helps you locate information on the World Wide Web. It uses a computer program called a **spider** to travel from one Web site to another, indexing the contents of the Web pages at each site based on **keywords**, or words that define your search topic. You can use a search engine to query these indexes to find Web pages containing the information you seek. Since the Web is constantly changing, the best search engine indexes are updated frequently. Table A-2 lists a number of factors that you need to consider in order to choose the search engine that's appropriate for your search.

► Search engines have limitations. For example, no single search engine indexes all of the Web. Therefore, no matter how well you define your search, a single search engine would find only a portion of the relevant Web pages. Also, because the Web changes daily, spiders are about six months behind in their indexing. As a result, newer Web pages and sites often won't be indexed yet.

► The search engine spiders that create the indexes are computer programs, not people. Due to the vagaries of the English language, many times your searches will find irrelevant results. For example, if you type the term *china* in a search engine, you might find information about Taiwan, the People's Republic of China, and porcelain cups and saucers as well.

► In the time it took you to read this lesson over 1,800 pages were added to the Web.

TABLE A-1: Web file formats and extensions

file type	file extension	file name
Web page	.html (.htm)	Hypertext Markup Language
	.xml	Extensible Markup Language
Documents	.doc	Word document
	.pdf	Portable Document Format
	.ps	PostScript format
Images	.gif	Graphics Interchange Format
	.jpg (.jpeg)	Joint Photographic Experts Group
	.tif (.tiff)	Tagged Image File Format
	.png	Portable Network Graphics
Audio	.au	Audio
	.aiff	Audio Interchange File Format
	.mp3	Moving Picture Experts Group Layer-3 Audio
	.ra	RealAudio
	.wav	Windows Audio Volume
Video	.avi	Audio Video Interleave
	.mov (.movie)	Quick Time movies
	.mpg (.mpeg)	Moving Picture Experts Group

TABLE A-2: Ways in which search engines differ

characteristic	explanation
Size	How much of the Web is indexed by the search engine's spider?
Scope	Does the engine index the Web in general or just a specialized area, like history or biology?
Formats	Does the search engine spider look only for Web (.html or .xml) pages, or does it also index image, audio, and video files?
Currency	How often is the search engine index updated?
Ways of searching	Can you enter a complete sentence in the search text box?
Results display	Does the search engine show only the title of the page in your results, or does it give additional information about the page as well?
Results ranking	How does the search engine rank (order) search results? Does the search engine accept payments from Web sites for preferential ranking? Does a large corporation own the site and rank the results in a way that might benefit the corporation?
Single vs. metasearch	Does the search engine search only its own index or does it search other indexes as well? A search engine that searches multiple search engines is called a **metasearch** engine.

Creating an Internet Research Strategy

The most important part of any search is the beginning, when you focus on what information you want to find and how you might find it. Typically, the biggest mistake an inexperienced searcher makes is sitting down at a computer and typing a single keyword in the first search engine encountered. This kind of search usually produces an overwhelming list of useless results. Creating an effective and efficient research strategy, however, can yield relevant, helpful results in an instant. Although no hard and fast search rules exist, the following eight steps provide guidelines that greatly increase the likelihood of finding what you are looking for in a timely manner. For an illustration of these steps, see Figure A-1. You are excited to begin looking for information about alternative energy sources. However, you realize that a few minutes spent developing a research strategy now will pay off in the long run.

Details

QuickTip

If you get stuck at any point in your research, call or visit a librarian. They are information experts.

▶ **Define your research topic**

Ask yourself what you want to end up with when you finish your research. Write down your topic. You don't have to use complete sentences. Phrases and words are fine, but be thorough.

▶ **Locate background information**

You may initially know very little about the topic you are researching. Look for general articles in encyclopedias and reference sources first. They will give you a good foundation for your research, and will also give you keywords to use in your search.

▶ **Decide where to look**

If you decide the World Wide Web is the best place to look for your topic, you will need to decide which area you want to look at. Ask yourself if you are looking for textual information on a Web page, an old e-mail or newsgroup posting, or maybe a graphic or an audio file. Knowing what format you are looking for will help determine which search tool you choose.

▶ **Choose the proper search tool**

There are many different ways to access information on the Web. Depending on what you are looking for, one tool may be better than another.

▶ **Translate your question into an effective search query**

The first step in translating a question into an effective search query is to identify the keywords that best describe the topic. You can use keywords to query a particular search engine or to query multiple search engines in a metasearch. For pinpoint accuracy, you can also use them to construct complex searches.

▶ **Perform your search**

Search engines offer a variety of different **search forms** where you can enter your query. Searching a subject guide, on the other hand, usually involves selecting a series of links to reach the information you seek.

▶ **Evaluate your search results**

The appearance, quantity, and quality of search results will vary from one search engine to another. To ascertain the value of the information you find, you will need to apply **evaluative criteria**, such as who authored the Web page, or how current the information is, to establish the quality of your results.

▶ **Refine your search (optional)**

Depending on the quality and quantity of your search results, you may need to go back to a previous step in the research process to refine your strategy. Use what you learned from your first pass through this process in your refined search. You may decide to use a different search tool, or maybe different keywords.

FIGURE A-1: The research process

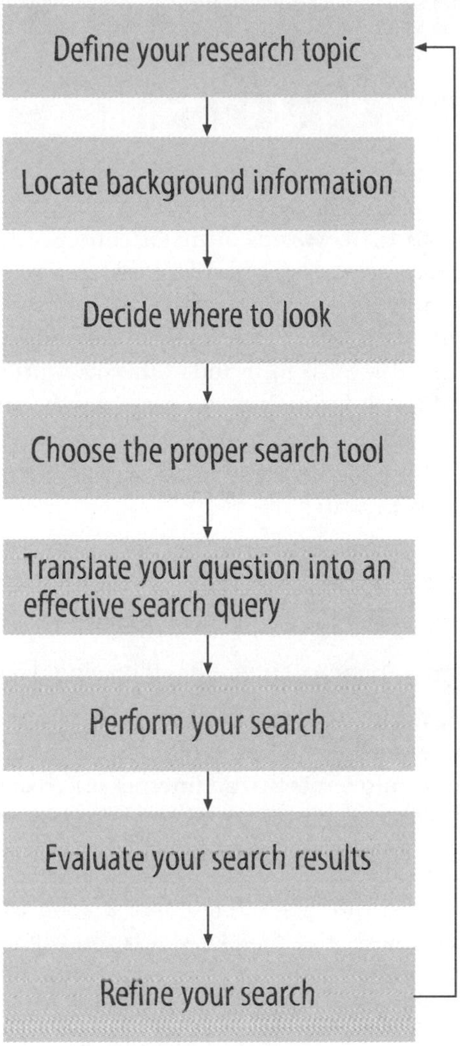

Define your research topic

↓

Locate background information

↓

Decide where to look

↓

Choose the proper search tool

↓

Translate your question into an effective search query

↓

Perform your search

↓

Evaluate your search results

↓

Refine your search

Choosing the proper search tool

If you are familiar with the topic you are researching, a search engine or metasearch engine allows you to quickly locate related Web pages. If you are unsure about the exact nature of the topic, then a **subject guide** lets you browse through relevant links arranged hierarchically by category. For specialty information, you may need to use dedicated directories, databases, **newsgroups** (archives of interactive Internet communication), or even **intelligent agents** (autonomous software programs that translate your search into the formats appropriate for multiple search engines, subject guides, and databases.) A **periodical database** is a specialized database that contains the full text of newspaper and magazine articles. Common periodical databases available at libraries are **ProQuest**, **InfoTrac**, and **EbscoHost**. This kind of database usually requires a paid subscription.

Finding the Right Keywords

Once you have identified your research topic, you need to translate it to a form that will optimize your chances of finding the information you seek. You can do this by focusing on your topic and pulling out the keywords or major concepts. Keywords are typically the nouns and verbs (and sometimes important adjectives) that describe your search topic. In the alternative energy example shown in Figure A-2, the initial keywords are *alternative, energy, solar, wind, water, biomass,* and *geothermal.* Once you have identified the keywords in your research topic, you must then expand the list to include other keywords with similar meanings. This step is important because the information you seek may be indexed under these other keywords. After thinking about your topic and consulting background information, you have identified the research topic shown in Figure A-2. You are now ready to define and expand the list of keywords for your search query.

1. **Copy the research topic from Figure A-2 onto a sheet of paper**
   Writing your topic down is a good way to focus.

2. **With a pen or a pencil, circle the following keywords in your topic: alternative, energy, solar, wind, water, biomass, geothermal**
   Notice that these words are all either nouns or adjectives. By circling them, you are starting to turn your topic into terms that an Internet search engine can use. Remember, these are the words you expect to appear on the Web pages that contain the information you seek. For a list of words that usually don't qualify as keywords, see Table A-3.

3. **Copy each keyword that you circled onto a separate line, as shown in Figure A-3**
   Now you can clearly see the main keywords you will use in your search.

4. **Adjacent to each keyword, write down the synonyms for the word, as shown in Figure A-4**
   Synonyms are words that have similar meanings. The meanings don't have to be exactly the same, just close. The Web pages you are looking for may be created by thousands of different people, using different words to describe your topic. By expanding your list of keywords, you help ensure that your search query will be broad enough to find the Web pages not indexed under the keywords in your initial list.

TABLE A-3: Parts of speech that usually do not make good keywords

part of speech	examples
Articles	a, an, the
Prepositions	in, of, about, on, in, above
Adverbs	probably, however, very
Some common verbs	is, see, do
Some common adjectives	quick, fine, happy

FIGURE A-2: Defining your research topic

I want to find information about sources of alternative energy. I am interested in the following types of alternative energy: solar, wind, water, biomass, and geothermal.

FIGURE A-3: Identifying keywords

I want to find information about sources of (alternative)(energy.) I am interested in the following types of alternative energy: (solar,)(wind,)(water,) (biomass) and (geothermal.)

Keywords

alternative
energy
solar
wind
water
biomass
geothermal

FIGURE A-4: Finding synonyms

I want to find information about sources of (alternative)(energy.) I am interested in the following types of alternative energy: (solar,)(wind,)(water,) (biomass) and (geothermal.)

Keywords	Synonyms		
alternative	renewable	sustainable	
energy	power		
solar	photovoltaic		
wind	turbines		
water	hydro	hydroelectric	hydropower
biomass	bioenergy		
geothermal			

Performing a Basic Search

Most search engines offer basic or simple searching at their Web sites. However, search engines often differ in how they perform basic searching, so you should view an engine's Help pages before you use it. An effective search statement at one search engine may produce poor results at another. You can overcome these inconsistencies by using a trial and error approach to searching. At each search engine, try subtle variations on a search, changing your wording slightly. Keep track of the wording that works best for a particular search engine. Also, record which search engines perform best for different kinds of searches, noting the ones that produce the greatest number of valuable results. Over time, you will learn which search engines give you the best results for different subjects. You decide to do some basic searching. You want to look for Web pages that give you information about solar energy.

Steps

1. Open the Project File **IR-A1.rtf** in your word processing program, then save it as **Searching the Internet.rtf**

This Project File will help you keep track of your search results. It is organized by lesson. You will use the same Project File throughout the lessons in this unit, switching between the Project File and your browser as necessary.

Trouble?

If AOL Search is not responding, the Student Online Companion will direct you to an alternative search engine.

2. Open your browser, go to the Student Online Companion at **www.course.com/illustrated/research**, then click the **AOL Search link** (under "Search engines")

The AOL search form appears, as shown in Figure A-5. You are now ready to enter your keywords.

QuickTip

Netscape Navigator users can turn the sidebar off by clicking My Sidebar on the View menu.

3. Click the **Search text box**, type **solar energy**, then click the **Search button**

After a few moments, your search results appear. Your screen should look similar to Figure A-6.

4. Scroll to see the number of results near the bottom of the page, then use the Project File to record how many Web pages this search found

Now you decide to alter the search by using the word *power* instead of *energy*.

5. Delete your previous query in the **Search text box**, type **solar power**, press **Enter**, then use the Project File to record how many Web pages this search found

Notice that your browser displays a different number of results for this search than the last. One small change in a search query can radically change the number and quality of search results. You know that using a different search engine can also change your results. You decide to try using Google.

6. Go to the Student Online Companion at **www.course.com/illustrated/research**, then click the **Google search link** (under "Search engines")

The search form for Google appears. You will now try your search queries at this search engine.

QuickTip

If you want to find the one site Google thinks is the "best," click the I'm Feeling Lucky button.

7. Click the **Search text box**, type **solar energy**, then click the **Google Search button**

After a few moments, your search results appear.

8. Use the Project File to record how many Web pages this search found, delete your previous query in the **Search text box**, type **solar power**, then click the **Google Search button**

Notice that again, the browser displays a different number of results for this search than the last.

9. Use the Project File to record how many Web pages this search found, answer the questions, then save the file

FIGURE A-5: AOL Search form

URL text box

Search text box

Search button

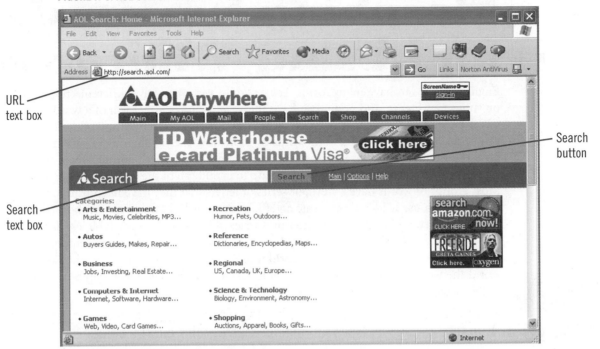

FIGURE A-6: AOL solar energy search results

Sponsored links

AOL disclaimer

Search results

Advertisements

Scroll down to see the number of search results below

Why do search results vary with different search engines?

When a search engine spider scans the Internet for Web pages, it finds only a fraction of the Web pages that exist for any given topic. Each search engine's spider finds different Web pages, so when you use a different search engine you are actually searching a slightly different part of the World Wide Web. That's why results can vary between search engines.

Morphing Keywords and Using Wildcards

English words can have many forms. For example, verbs can have different endings, depending on subject and tense, and nouns can have alternate spellings. Any form of a word may appear on a Web page. When you construct an Internet search, you have to be aware of these variations. You can find spelling variants for your words by **morphing** them. Obvious variations to include are both the singular and plural forms of a noun, and different verb endings for a verb. Morphing keywords does not necessarily mean you have to include all of the word variations in your search. Most groups of words have a **stem**, or series of letters that they have in common. If you find this stem, you can use wildcards to create an efficient search. **Wildcards** are symbols (for example, *, ?, or %) that stand in for a single letter or a series of letters in a word. Table A-4 lists some examples of stems with wildcards. You want to look up solar energy centers not just in the United States, but in the rest of the world too. You realize that in much of the English-speaking world the word *center* is spelled *centre*. You decide to formulate your search using wildcards in order to get international results.

Steps

1. In the Project File, type your original search, **solar energy center**

2. In the table cell beneath the word **center**, type the international variant **centre** and the plural forms **centers** and **centres**, as shown in Figure A-7

You have now morphed your original keyword center by identifying its variant forms. You realize this step is necessary because Web pages might contain any combination of the words *solar energy center*, *solar energy centers*, *solar energy centre*, or *solar energy centres*.

3. In the cell beneath your list of words, starting from the left, type each letter that these words have in common: **c-e-n-t**

You now have identified the stem. Truncating is another word to describe what you have just done. **Truncating** means cutting off the part of the word beyond the stem.

4. In the next cell, type the stem followed by the wildcard symbol *: **cent***

The wildcard symbol * replaces all of the letters that you truncated in the step above. The keyword *cent** will find all of the spelling variations—center, centers, centre, and centres.

5. In the next cell down, type the new morphed search words, **solar energy cent***

6. Go to the Student Online Companion at **www.course.com/illustrated/research**, then click the **AltaVista link** (under "Search engines")

The search form for the AltaVista search engine appears. You are now ready to enter your morphed search.

7. Click the **Search for text box**, type **solar energy cent***, click the **Search button**, then use the Project File to record how many Web pages this search found

After a few moments, your search results appear. Your screen should look similar to Figure A-8. Now you want to compare your morphed search results to your original search.

8. Delete your previous query, type **solar energy center** in the **Search for text box**, then click the **Search button**

Notice that this search yields fewer results than the last. This search found only Web pages with the words *solar energy center*; not *solar energy centre*, *solar energy centers*, or *solar energy centres*.

9. Record the number of search results in the Project File, then save the file

FIGURE A-7: Morphing the word center

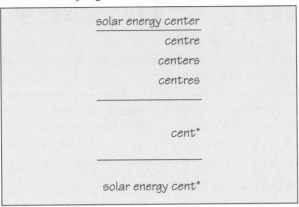

solar energy center

centre

centers

centres

cent*

solar energy cent*

FIGURE A-8: AltaVista Search solar energy cent*

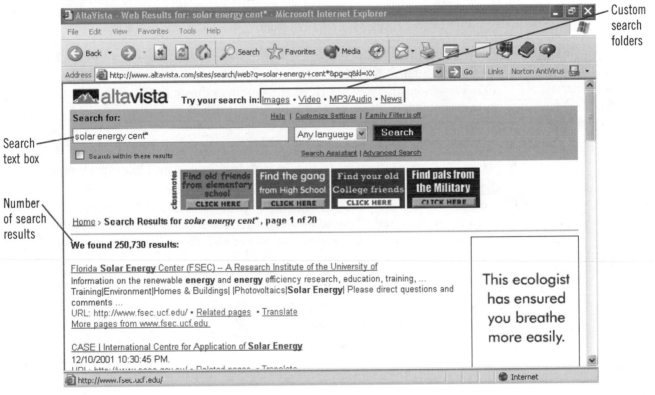

TABLE A-4: Examples of morphing keywords and using wildcards

morphable words	morphs	stem with wildcard
Plural nouns	supply, supplies, supplier, suppliers	suppl*
	woman, women	wom*n
Verb endings	grow, grows, growing	grow*
Variant spellings	color, colour	col*r

(Note: Wildcard symbols vary from search engine to search engine, and their meaning may vary depending on their position at the beginning, middle, or end of a word. The asterisk used here is just an example.)

Using Phrases

When you construct a search, you are often looking for two or more words to be in a sentence or phrase one right after the other. In order to find your words in just the right order you will want to use **phrase searching**. At many search engines, phrase searching is accomplished by putting quotation marks (" ") around the block of words you want to appear together on the Web pages the search engine returns. You realize that your search can be refined even more with phrase searching. You decide to try a few more searches and compare the results.

Steps

1. Go to the Student Online Companion at **www.course.com/illustrated/research**, then click the **Google link** (under "Search engines")

   The search form for the Google search engine appears. You are now ready to enter your search.

2. Click the **Google Search text box**, type **bioenergy center**, then click the **Google Search button**

   After a few moments, your search results appear, as shown in Figure A-9.

3. Use the Project File to record the number of results this search found

   You want to try a similar search, with a different word order, to see how the results differ.

4. Delete your previous query in the **Search text box**, type **center bioenergy**, then click the **Google Search button**

   After a few moments, your search results appear, as shown in Figure A-10. You should have the same number of results as in your previous search. If *center bioenergy* and *bioenergy center* find the same number of results, then you haven't yet limited your search to just the phrase *bioenergy center*. You decide to use phrase searching to limit your results.

5. Delete your previous query in the **Search text box**, type **"bioenergy center"**, then click the **Google Search button**

   Make sure you use the quotation marks around these words as shown in Figure A-11 in order to search for the phrase "bioenergy center." You should now have far fewer results than in either of your first two searches. You have located only the Web pages that contain the phrase *bioenergy center*.

6. Use the Project File to record your results, answer the questions, then save the Project File

CLUES TO USE

Other ways to search using phrases

Most search engines allow phrase searching, but not all use quotation marks around a group of words to indicate a phrase. Some search engines automatically assume you are looking for a phrase when you type two words right next to each other in the Search text box. At those search engines the quotation marks would be redundant, but harmless. Some search engines provide a drop-down menu or check box with the option for the "exact phrase." Others include an additional Search text box titled "with this exact phrase" on an advanced search page. Use the Help or Search Tip pages available at the search engine site to find out exactly how to use phrase searching.

FIGURE A-9: Searching for the keywords bioenergy center

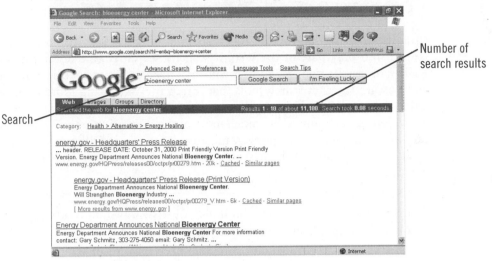

Search

Number of search results

FIGURE A-10: Searching for the keywords center bioenergy

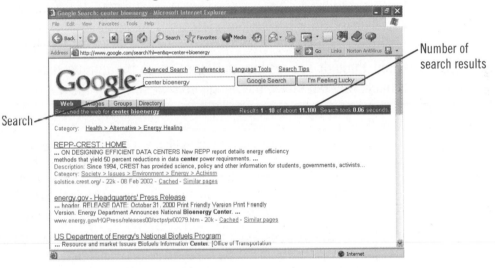

Search

Number of search results

FIGURE A-11: Searching for the phrase "bioenergy center"

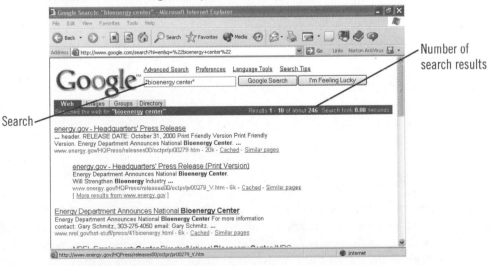

Search

Number of search results

Metasearching

Up until now each of your searches has used only a single search engine. At best you have tapped into only part of the Web. If a single search engine doesn't deliver the number or quality of results you need, then you may need to use a metasearch engine. **Metasearch engines** are Internet search tools that search the Web using more than one search engine's index, as shown in Table A-5. Because of this ability to do many parallel searches simultaneously, you can actually access much more of the Web using a good metasearch engine. As you can see from Table A-6, however, metasearching is not without its downside. You want to locate some Web sites on geothermal energy. You decide to try searching with a metasearch engine.

Steps

1. Go to the Student Online Companion at **www.course.com/illustrated/research**, then click the **Ixquick link** (under "Metasearch engines")

The metasearch form Ixquick appears. You are now ready to enter your search.

2. Click the **Search text box**, type **"geothermal energy"**, then click the **Search button**

Your search is now simultaneously sent to many search engines including AOL, AltaVista, Excite, FindWhat, LookSmart, MSN, and Yahoo. Ixquick, along with ProFusion, is one of only a few "smart" metasearch engines. It translates unique search commands, like the quotation marks that indicate phrase searching, into queries that other search engines understand.

3. Scroll through the results, noting some of the unique results display features of Ixquick: **ranking stars**, the **Highlighted Result**, and the **list of search engines** after each result

Your Ixquick search results should look similar to Figure A-12. Ixquick uses stars to rank your search results by relevance. The Highlighted Result link takes you to a copy of the Web page, with your search terms highlighted for easy scanning. At the bottom of each Web page in the list, Ixquick indicates how each search engine ranked that page. Also note the "Sponsored Link" notation for the first search result. This is the way Ixquick lets you know which Web sites have paid for placement.

4. Scroll down the page of results, if necessary, then click the words **Highlighted Result**

This copy of the Web page has the words in your search query highlighted. This feature can help you determine how useful the Web page might be.

5. In the Project File, list three of the Web sites your search yielded, then save the file

CLUES TO USE

Maximizing metasearching

You need to keep a few things in mind when you use a metasearch engine. First, read the Help pages provided by the engine. Help will let you know how "smart" the engine is in translating specific search commands into queries that other search engines understand. If you have this information, you will know if it makes sense to use wildcards like the asterisk * or quotation marks to indicate a phrase. If you're not sure how smart the metasearch engine is, use simple searches consisting of only a few keywords.

FIGURE A-12: Ixquick metasearch results

Sponsored result

Highlighted result

List of search engines with their ranking of this page

Number of search results

Ranking stars

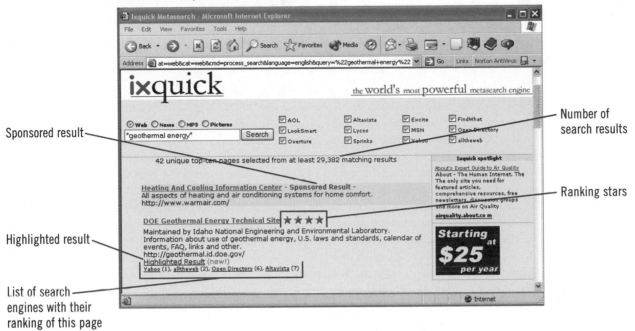

TABLE A-5: Metasearch engines

metasearch engine	other search engines and directories queried
Ixquick	AOL AltaVista Excite Yahoo! FindWhat GoTo LookSmart MSN
Search.com	LookSmart Yahoo! OpenDirectory Teoma
Dogpile	GoTo LookSmart FindWhat Direct Hit AltaVista Open Directory Yahoo!
MetaCrawler	AltaVista DirectHit Excite FindWhat Google GoTo.com LookSmart WebCrawler
ProFusion	About All the Web AOL Excite Lycos Yahoo! AltaVista LookSmart MSN

TABLE A-6: Pitfalls of metasearch engines

metasearch pitfall	explanation
Might not include the "best" search engine	Many of the best search engines will charge metasearch engines to use them, so they often don't.
Unstable	Search engines come and go quickly and metasearch engines add and drop them from their lists frequently. The engines that gave you good results last week might no longer be included in your metasearch.
Inconsistent	Doing the same search query a few seconds apart can achieve radically different results. If a search engine is busy, your metasearch might ignore it this time - and you won't find the Web sites you found a few minutes ago.
Limited to simple keyword searches	More complex search commands are not translated into the proper query at every **keyword searches** search engine. While an asterisk ($*$) may indicate a wildcard at some search engines, others may use the percentage sign (%) or question mark (?) as the substitute for a single character or multiple characters, respectively.
They are all different	Like individual search engines, metasearch engines all have their own idiosyncrasies. You should read the Help pages at each engine to find out how to use them effectively.

Citing Online Resources

Once you find good Internet sources you will want to keep track of them using either Internet Explorer's **Favorites** function or Netscape's **Bookmarks.** You may also need to use information on some of the Web pages you find as sources for school assignments or papers, in which case you will be typing up a list of works cited. You will need to gather enough information about each Web site so that you can get back to it at a later date, and also so that you can share these sites with your friends and colleagues. In order to make sure all the relevant data about each site is organized and consistent, you should adopt a citation format. **Citation formats** are style guides that standardize how citations are written. Two widely accepted citation formats are those of the Modern Language Association (MLA) and the American Psychological Association (APA). These style guides have different citation formats for different kinds of Internet information, from e-mail postings to image files. Always check with your instructor to see which style guide he or she prefers. ➤ You decide to use the MLA format to record your citations for the Web pages you are finding about alternative energy.

Steps

1. Review the MLA citation format in Figure A-13

Figure A-13 includes the elements you need to properly cite a generic Web page. You can use this information to cite the Web page shown in Figure A-14. Different kinds of materials on the Web have slightly different citation formats. Go to the Student Online Companion at www.course.com/illustrated/research to see a list of citation guide links.

Trouble?

Can't find the author's name? Then skip it and go right to the title of the Web page. Some Web pages don't acknowledge an author. For other citation tips, see Table A-7.

2. Looking at Figure A-15, locate the author and type his name in the Project File

MLA format for author names is the surname first followed by a comma, then the personal name followed by a period.

3. Locate the title of the Web page in Figure A-15 and type it next to the author's name

MLA format has you put quotation marks around the title and end the title with a period.

4. Find the general title of the Web site and type it next to the Web page title

The Web site title should be underlined and followed by a period.

5. Look for the date the Web page was created or the date it was last updated

Looking at the Web page in Figure A-15, you find no creation date or date last updated. There may be times when you must skip this step.

QuickTip

Notice that this URL has a .org extension in its domain name, which means that it is maintained by a non-profit organization. You can be pretty sure the article will not try to sell you a particular commercial product, though it may try to sell you an opinion.

6. Locate the Web page address (URL) in the URL text box, then type it next to the Web site title, < http://www.caddet-re.org/html/499art1.htm>

The URL should be enclosed in angle brackets < >; it should not be underlined.

7. Type the date that you are viewing this Web page (today's date) next, for example, 23 Oct. 2002

The MLA format for dates is *DD Month Abbreviation YYYY* followed by a period. Web pages are updated and changed so frequently that the date that you view the Web page is important to record. The information you saw last week might no longer be there.

8. Compare your citation to the completed example in Figure A-14, make corrections as needed, add your name to the Project File, then save, print, and close the Project File

Make sure you have used quotation marks and have underlined the right words. You must also include all of the required punctuation.

FIGURE A-13: MLA citation format for a generic Web page

Author last name, author first name.
"Web page title." <u>Web site title</u>.
Date created or revised.
<Full Internet address>
Date you viewed the Web page.

FIGURE A-14: Finished Web page citation

De Spiegeleer, E."The Power of Organic Wastes."
<u>Caddet Renewable Energy</u>.
<http://www.caddet-re.org./html/499art1.htm>
23 Oct. 2002.

FIGURE A-15: Web page for citation

URL (Web page address)
Web site title
Web page title
Author

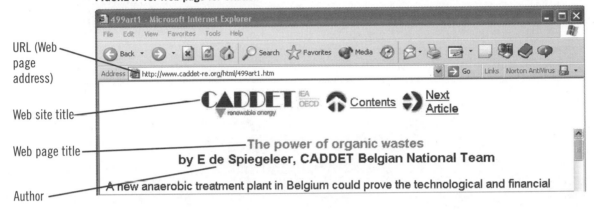

TABLE A-7: Citation tips

citation section	tip
Author	When authors aren't named on Web pages, skip the author section. Sometimes there is no individual author, just a **corporate author** (a committee, association, or government agency, like the U.S. Department of Agriculture). Make sure to include the corporate author in the author section of the citation.
Web page title	If you are citing the whole Web site, not just an individual page at that site, you can skip this section.
Creation or revision date	These dates can be hard to find. Look at the bottom of the Web page for them.
URL	Some word processors underline any URL you type. For the proper format, remove the underline.
Date viewed	If you print a copy of a Web page, the date you viewed it will be at the bottom right-hand corner.

CLUES TO USE

Copyright and plagiarism

Assume that everything you find on the Internet, whether it is a Web page, an image, or an audio file, is copyrighted. What does that mean to you?

If you are in a business and want to make money using a part of someone else's work, you must get permission from the author or creator. Copyright law is very complex, so you will want to use a lawyer who specializes in copyright law to help you.

If you are a student and wish to use part of someone else's work in a school report or paper you generally can, under the "Fair Use" exemption to copyright law. This law allows students and researchers to copy or use small parts of other people's creations or writings for educational purposes. However, you always must give credit by citing the source of the material you are using. If you use a fact, quotation, or image from the World Wide Web, you must briefly cite the source of your material in your paper, and give the full citation to the source on your List of Works Cited page. If you don't credit an author, you are guilty of plagiarism.

See the links to Copyright and Plagiarism in the Student Online Companion at www.course.com/illustrated/research for more information.

Practice

► Concepts Review

Label each element of Figure A-16.

FIGURE A-16

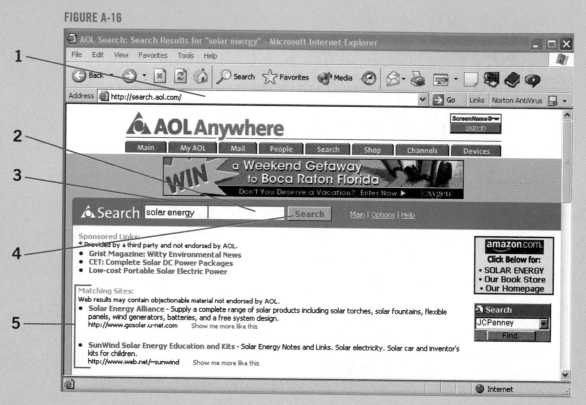

Match each of the following terms with the statement that describes its function.

6. WWW
7. GIF
8. Search engine
9. .html
10. Metasearch engine
11. The research process
12. Synonyms
13. Morphing
14. Wildcard

a. A Web site that helps you locate Internet information
b. Hypertext Markup Language
c. A search engine that searches multiple search engines
d. Symbols that stand in for a character or group of characters
e. Finding spelling variants for words
f. The World Wide Web
g. An image format
h. Words that have similar meanings
i. Guidelines that help you create a search strategy

Select the best answer from the following list of choices.

15. The Internet is:
a. The same as the World Wide Web.
b. A network of networks sharing a common communication standard.
c. Relatively small and decreasing in size every day.
d. Not an interactive medium.

16. The World Wide Web:
a. Is a collection of documents and media linked together over the Internet.
b. Only consists of documents with the .html extension.
c. Is the same as the Internet.
d. Does not include images, audio, or video files.

17. Which of the following is an extension for an image file on the WWW?
a. .au
b. .mp3
c. .jpeg
d. .wav

18. Which is the proper search tool for an Internet search?
a. An Internet Search engine
b. A metasearch engine
c. The tool varies depending on what you are looking for
d. A spider

19. Which is NOT a step in the research process?
a. Defining your research topic
b. Choosing the proper Internet search tool
c. Typing randomly without preparation
d. Evaluating your search results

20. In order to find any of the words child, child's, children, or children's, which is the best search?
a. child*
b. childr*
c. childs*
d. chil*

21. Phrase searching helps you find:
a. Words in the order you specify.
b. Keywords.
c. Wildcards.
d. Synonyms.

22. Which is NOT a pitfall of most metasearch engines?
   a. Instability
   b. Secrecy
   c. Inconsistency
   d. Limited to simple searching

23. Which is NOT part of an MLA citation for a generic Web page?
   a. Author's first name
   b. Web page title
   c. City where Web page is located
   d. URL

► Skills Review

1. Describe some features of the Internet or Internet Search engines.
   a. Open the Project File called SR-A.rtf, type your name in the space provided, and save it as **IR Skills Review-A.rtf**.
   b. Use the Project File to write a short paragraph describing three features of Internet Search engines.
   c. Save the Project File.

2. Review the research process.
   a. In the Project File, type the eight steps of the research process in order.
   b. Choosing three of the eight steps to focus on, use the Project File to write a short paragraph about why these steps are important to creating an effective search strategy.
   c. Save the Project File.

3. Find the right keywords.
   a. You have defined your search topic as follows: "I want to find information about the history of cotton farming."
   b. Type the topic in the Project File.
   c. Boldface or underline the three keywords in the topic.
   d. List the three keywords below the topic.
   e. Think of at least three synonyms for the keywords (not three for each of the keywords, just three synonyms total - they might all be synonyms for the same keyword).
   f. Use the Project File to enter the synonyms next to the appropriate keywords.
   g. Save the Project File.

4. Perform a basic search.
   a. You have determined your search query to be **cotton plantations**.
   b. Open your Internet browser.
   c. Go to the Student Online Companion at www.course.com/illustrated/research, and click the link for the Google search engine.
   d. Perform the search **cotton plantations**.
   e. Note the number of search results in the Project File.
   f. Save the Project File.

5. Morph keywords and use wildcards.

a. You have determined you want to find information about **cotton plants** and **cotton planting**.

b. Use the Project File to find and enter the stem common to both words.

c. Type the stem in the appropriate cell in the Project File.

d. Add the wildcard ∗ to the stem, and type it in the appropriate cell in the Project File.

e. Go to the Student Online Companion at www.course.com/illustrated/research, and click the link for AltaVista.

f. Execute the search, then enter the number of search results in the appropriate cell in the Project File.

g. Save the Project File.

6. Use a phrase in a search.

a. You have determined your search query to be **cotton plantations**.

b. Go to the Student Online Companion at www.course.com/illustrated/research, and click the link for the Google search engine.

c. Perform the search **cotton plantations**.

d. Use the Project File to record the number of search results.

e. Now search for the phrase **cotton plantations** by adding quotation marks.

f. Use the Project File to record the number of search results.

g. Save the Project File.

7. Perform a metasearch.

a. Use the Student Online Companion at www.course.com/illustrated/research to go to ixquick.

b. Search for the phrase **cotton plantations**.

c. On the resulting Ixquick search results page, look at one of the search results.

d. In the Project File, note a special feature that appears at the search result.

e. Use the Project File to record the number of search results on your paper.

f. Save the Project File.

8. Cite an online source.

a. Use the Project File to write down the six elements that must appear in an MLA format generic Web page citation.

b. Boldface the two elements that sometimes are hard to find on the Web page, and may be omitted.

c. Save the Project File and then print it.

Independent Challenge 1

You have determined that you want to find information on the Internet about skiing in British Columbia. You will try a few different searches to see which finds the best information.

a. Go to the Student Online Companion at www.course.com/illustrated/research, and click the link for the Google search engine.

b. Perform the keyword search **ski British Columbia**.

c. Record the number of search results in a text file with your name at the top, and save it as **Unit A IC1.rtf**.

d. Perform the keyword search **British Columbia skiing**.

e. Use the text file to record the number of search results.

f. Perform the phrase search **"British Columbia skiing"**.

g. Use the text file to record the number of search results.

h. Write a few sentences explaining which search you thought was the best and why the phrase search found far fewer results.

i. Add your name to the file, save it, and print it.

 # Independent Challenge 2

You are considering a career change and want to do a Web search. Your topic is "I want to find information about careers in computing in Great Britain."

a. Type the topic in a text editor or word processor and save it as **Unit A IC2.rtf**.

b. Boldface or underline the keywords in the topic.

c. Copy each keyword on to a separate line.

d. Adjacent to each keyword, type all of the synonyms you can think of.

e. Choose one of the keywords to morph, then type it at the bottom of the list.

f. Morph the word you chose, finding as many variants as you can, then type the variants next to the word.

g. Find the stem that is common to all of the variants, then type it on the next line.

h. On the next line, retype the stem, then add the wild card.

i. From all of your keywords, compose a search and type it on the next line (make sure to include the morphed word with its wildcard in the search).

j. Go to the Student Online Companion at www.course.com/illustrated/research, then click the link for AltaVista.

k. Perform your search, then type the number of search results in your file.

l. Add your name to the file, save it, and print it.

Independent Challenge 3

You want to find information on the Internet.

   a. Decide on a topic and write it down in a sentence or two on a piece of blank paper.

   b. Decide what the keywords are and identify synonyms for them.

   c. Compose a search query, choose a search engine, and perform a search.

   d. Look at the number of search results you received, and decide if the number seems appropriate.

   e. If you need to, refine your search and compose a different search query or go to another search engine and perform your search.

   f. When you are satisfied with your search results, print the first page of the search results and write your name on the top.

 # Independent Challenge 4

You want to get to know how search engines work. You decide to choose a topic and compare search results.

   a. Decide on a topic and write it down in a sentence or two in a text file that you save as **Unit A IC4.rtf**.

   b. Decide what the keywords are in your topic and boldface them.

   c. Use a table to record each of the keywords and its synonyms.

   d. Decide which of the keywords you want to search with and go to **www.ixquick.com** and then to **www.search.msn.com** and perform the same keyword search at each.

   e. Use the Project File to record the number of results at each search engine.

   f. Choose two of your keywords that are a phrase and try a phrase search (putting quotation marks around the words) at both **www.ixquick.com** and **www.search.msn.com**.

   g. Use the Project File to record the number of search results from each search engine.

   h. Using the Help pages, read a little about searching at both Ixquick and MSN Search.

   i. In the same Project File, write a paragraph explaining why the search engines' results are different.

   j. Add your name to the file, then save and print the file.

► Visual Workshop

You found this great bonsai Web page and want to record the relevant information from it so you can refer to it in the future. You will use the MLA citation format for a generic Web page. In a text editor or in your word processing software, write the citation for this Web page. Add your name to the file, save it as Unit A VW.rtf, then print the file.

FIGURE A-17

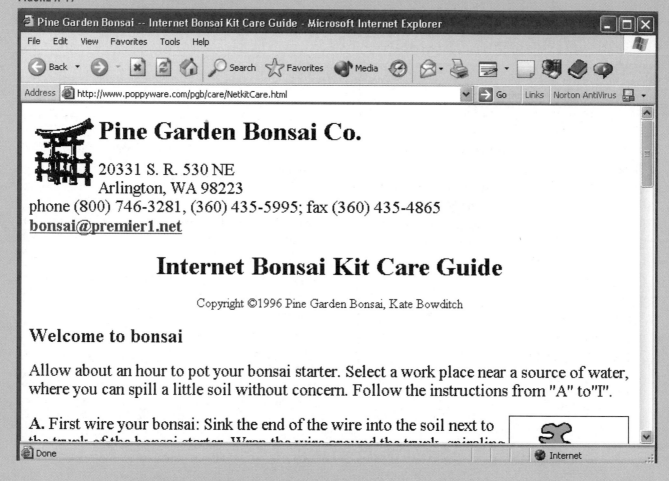

Unit
B

Constructing
Deep Searches

Objectives

► **Understand Boolean operators**
► **Narrow the search with the AND operator**
► **Expand the search with the OR operator**
► **Restrict queries with the AND NOT operator**
► **Search by proximity with NEAR/ and W/ operators**
► **Combine operators for power searches**
► **Search with filters**
► **Analyze search results**

In the previous unit, you learned how to perform a basic search using keywords, wildcards, and phrases. However, many search engines offer the ability to construct more complex query statements. A **complex query** uses special connecting words and symbols called Boolean operators to define the relationships between your keywords and phrases. **Boolean operators**, such as AND, OR, and AND NOT, let you expand, narrow, or restrict your searches based on Boolean logic. **Boolean logic**, or Boolean algebra, is the field of mathematics that defines how Boolean operators manipulate large sets of data. Since search engines handle large data sets, most of them support Boolean logic and complex query statements. In addition, **search filters** provide another method to narrow your search by limiting its scope to a specific part of the Web. Combining complex query statements with search filters lets you conduct a deep search in order to focus on finding exactly what you are looking for. So far your searches for information about alternative energy have retrieved lots of results, but not the exact information you need. To achieve more precise results, you decide to use Boolean operators and filters to refine and focus your search.

Understanding Boolean Operators

The English language has a set of rules, or syntax, for combining words to form grammatical sentences. Many search engines rely on a special mathematical syntax or set of rules—called Boolean logic—for constructing proper complex queries. In Boolean logic, keywords act like the nouns in an English sentence. Like nouns, keywords are the concrete things that comprise your subject. Boolean operators are like the conjunctions in an English sentence: They define the connections between different keywords in a complex query. In order to use search engines more effectively, you decide to spend some time learning about Boolean operators.

► Common Boolean operators

The most common Boolean operators are the words AND, OR, and AND NOT. You can use them in your search query to connect keywords and phrases in meaningful ways. When included in your search, they act as commands to the search engine. They tell the engine which keywords *must* be on the Web page; which *may* be on the Web page (but don't have to be); and which *must not* be on the Web page.

► Proximity operators

Other Boolean operators are called proximity operators. **Proximity operators** tell a search engine how close keywords should be to each other on a Web page. The quotation marks you used in phrase searching in Unit A function as proximity operators: By putting quotes around two or more keywords, you command the search engine to find the keywords in exactly the order you enter them, one right after the other on a Web page. Other proximity operators, which can specify the number of words or symbols between two or more keywords on a page, are NEAR/ and W/ (within).

► Venn diagrams

A way to visualize how Boolean operators work is by using drawings called **Venn diagrams**. For example, imagine that all of the Web pages on the World Wide Web can be represented by the rectangle shown in Figures B-1 to B-4. Circles inside the rectangle represent groups of related Web pages, called **sets**. The circle in Figure B-1 represents all of the Web pages that contain the word *wind*. One circle in Figure B-2 represents the set of Web pages that contain the word *wind*, and the other circle represents the set of Web pages that contain the word *turbine*.

► Intersection and union

The shaded section in Figure B-3, where the two circles overlap, is called the **intersection** of the two sets; in Boolean terms this section would include Web pages that contain both words. The shaded section of Figure B-4 is called the **union** of the two sets. It represents all of the Web pages containing the word *wind* combined with all of the Web pages containing the word *turbine*.

► Where to use Boolean operators

Some search engines allow Boolean searching at the basic search page; others allow it only at the advanced or "power" search page. Often the advanced search page will have pull-down menus that have options for AND, OR, or AND NOT. If you are unsure how to use Boolean searching at a new search engine, or unsure if it is even allowed, use the search engine's Help pages.

► Default Boolean operator

Each search engine inserts Boolean operators in your searches, whether you supply them in the search query or not. The Boolean term that the search engine uses for your query is called the **default operator**. Most search engines default to the AND operator, although a few default to the OR operator. When you put two or more terms in a Search text box at some search engines, they automatically assume you want to find the words one right after the other in a phrase, and so supply quotation marks around your words. Other search engines treat each word as a separate keyword. Knowing that search engines insert these Boolean terms automatically, and knowing how to use Boolean operators, will greatly increase your chances of quickly finding relevant information on the Web.

FIGURE B-1: Diagram representing Web pages that contain the word wind

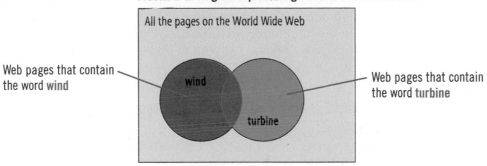

All the pages on the World Wide Web

Web pages that contain the word wind

wind

Web pages that *don't* contain the word wind

FIGURE B-2: Diagram representing the sets wind and turbine

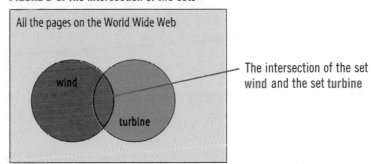

All the pages on the World Wide Web

Web pages that contain the word wind

wind

turbine

Web pages that contain the word turbine

FIGURE B-3: The intersection of two sets

All the pages on the World Wide Web

wind

turbine

The intersection of the set wind and the set turbine

FIGURE B-4: The union of two sets

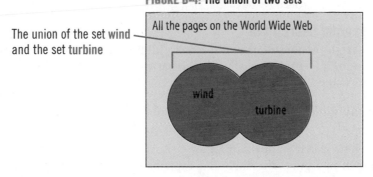

The union of the set wind and the set turbine

All the pages on the World Wide Web

wind

turbine

CLUES TO USE

Where have you heard this before?

You might remember Boolean logic and Venn diagrams from math class. George Boole (1815-1864), an Englishman, invented a form of symbolic logic called Boolean Algebra, which is used in the fields of mathematics, logic, computer science, and artificial intelligence today. John Venn (1843-1923), also an Englishman, used his diagrams to explain visually what Boole had described symbolically—the intersection, union, and exclusion of sets. Little did they know in the 1800s that they were helping to create the foundation of the language Internet search engines use today.

Narrowing the Search with the AND Operator

The Boolean operator AND is a powerful term. Whenever you connect keywords in your search with AND, you are commanding the search engine to find *both* of the keywords on the same Web page. Each time you add another AND to your search, you are further narrowing the search. As a result, the search engine will return fewer and fewer Web pages. However, the Web pages the search does return will be more relevant than those returned by a less specific search. In other words, the best time to use AND is when your initial keyword or phrase search finds too many irrelevant results. ◄────── You want to find out if there are any solar energy associations near you in Portland.

1. Open the Project File **IR-B1.rtf** in your word processing program, then save it as **Deep Searches.rtf**

   This document contains a table that you can use to record your search results.

2. Open your browser, go to the Student Online Companion at **www.course.com/illustrated/research**, click the **MSN Search link**, then click the **Advanced Search tab**

   The MSN Advanced Search page appears, as shown in Figure B-5. You are now ready to search. Boolean operators are not allowed in MSN basic searches. In order to perform this kind of deep search, you need to use the Advanced Search page. Notice the "Advanced Search Options" on the page. These are alternative ways of performing Boolean searches.

3. Type **"solar energy association"** in the Search text box, then click the **Search button**

   After a few moments, your search results appear. They are illustrated in the Venn diagram shown in Figure B-6.

4. Use the Project File to record how many Web pages this search found

   Keeping track of the number of results will help you see how the different Boolean operators can broaden or narrow a search.

5. Click the **Advanced Search tab**

   Your original search should still be in the Search text box on the Advanced Search page. The search found many Web pages, but you want to narrow your results to just *Portland*. You can accomplish this using the AND operator.

6. Type **"solar energy association" AND Portland** in the Search text box, then click the **Search button**

   A diagram of your search is shown in Figure B-7. After a few moments, your search results appear, as shown in Figure B-8. Table B-1 explains how the AND operator affected your results. Note that the results for this search are found at the intersection of the two sets.

7. Use the Project File to record how many Web pages this search found, then answer the question for this lesson

   You have successfully narrowed your search to include only Web pages that include both the phrase "*solar energy association*" and the word *Portland*.

8. Type **Your Name** at the top of the Deep Searches document, then save the document

FIGURE B-5: MSN Advanced search page

MSN Advanced — search URL

MSN Advanced — Search page

Advanced Search tab

Advanced — search options

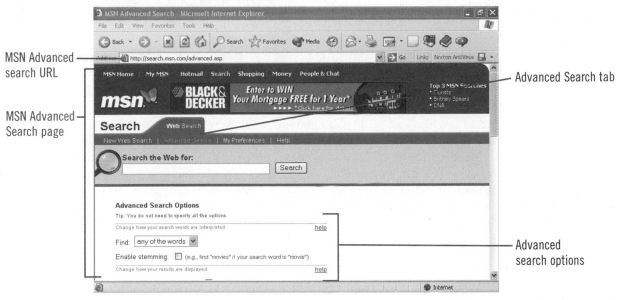

FIGURE B-6: Diagram of "solar energy association" search

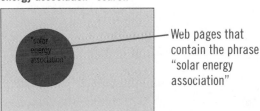

Web pages that contain the phrase "solar energy association"

Web pages that contain **both** the phrase "solar energy association" AND Portland (the intersection of these two sets)

FIGURE B-7: Diagram of "solar energy association" AND Portland search

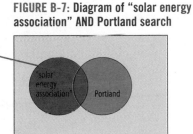

FIGURE B-8: MSN Advanced "solar energy association" AND Portland search

Search text box

Number of search results, followed by your search query

TABLE B-1: The AND operator

when to use AND	variations of AND at some search engines	advanced searching and AND	search phrase and results
• When you are finding too many results • In order to make your search more specific	• and (lowercase) • + (the plus sign)	Some search engines allow AND searching at their advanced search pages. They may have pull-down menus or check boxes with words like: • Must include • All of the words • Must contain	"solar energy" AND "photovoltaic panels" Entering this text in a Search text box would find all Web pages that include **both** phrases.

Internet Research

Expanding the Search with the OR Operator

The Boolean operator OR is also a powerful term. Whenever you connect keywords in your search with OR, you are commanding the search engine to find *either* of the keywords on a Web page. Therefore, each time you add another OR to your search, you are expanding the search to include more Web pages. A good time to use OR is when your initial keyword or phrase search finds too few results. Think of synonyms for your keyword or phrase, and add them to your search with a connecting OR. See Table B-2 for more information about the OR operator. You want to find Web pages that contain the words *wind turbines* or *wind energy*. You are not sure which one of these phrases will give you the better search results.

Steps

Trouble?

If you are not at the MSN Search site, go to the Student Online Companion at *www.course.com/illustrated/ research* and click the MSN Search link.

1. At the MSN Search site, click the **Advanced Search tab**

You are now ready to search by connecting two keyword phrases with the OR operator. First, however, you try one phrase without the other.

2. Delete your previous query, type **"wind turbines"** in the Search text box, then click the **Search button**

After a few moments, your search results appear. A Venn diagram illustrating your search is shown in Figure B-9.

3. Use the Project File to record how many Web pages this search found

4. Click the **Advanced Search tab**, delete your previous query from the Search text box, type **"wind energy"**, then click the **Search button**

After a few moments, your search results appear. A Venn diagram illustrating your search is shown in Figure B-10.

5. Use the Project File to record how many Web pages this search found

Now you want to see how many results you get if you connect the two search phrases using the OR operator.

6. Click the **Advanced Search tab**, delete your previous query in the Search text box, type **"wind turbines" OR "wind energy"**, then click the **Search button**

A Venn diagram illustrating your search results is shown in Figure B-11. Notice that this search combined the results of both of the other searches. However, the number of search results for this search is not what you might expect. Instead of the number of results representing the sum of the other result sets, it is somewhat lower. This difference can be attributed to the fact that some of the Web pages have both of the phrases *"wind turbines"* and *"wind energy"* on them.

QuickTip

If you are using a metasearch engine, always use all capital letters when typing any Boolean operator. All search engines that allow Boolean searching will understand OR, while some may not be able to interpret *or* as the Boolean operator OR.

7. Use the Project File to record how many Web pages this search found, answer the question for this lesson, then save the document

You have successfully expanded your search to include Web pages that contain either the phrase *"wind turbines"* or *"wind energy."*

FIGURE B-9: Diagram of "wind turbines" search

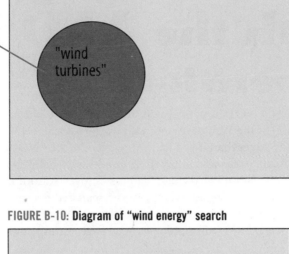

Web pages that contain the phrase *"wind turbines"*

"wind turbines"

FIGURE B-10: Diagram of "wind energy" search

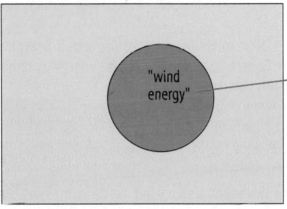

"wind energy"

Web pages that contain the phrase *"wind energy"*

FIGURE B-11: Diagram of "wind turbines" OR "wind energy" search

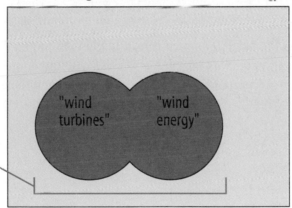

"wind turbines"

"wind energy"

Web pages that contain either the phrase *"wind turbines"* OR *"wind energy"*

TABLE B-2: The OR operator

when to use OR	variation of OR at some search engines	advanced searching and OR	search phrase and results
• When you are finding too few results • In order to make your search more broad • To combine synonyms	• or (no capital letters)	Some search engines allow OR searching at their advanced search pages. They may have pull-down menus or check boxes with words like: • Any of the words • Some of the words	"energy conservation" OR "energy efficiency" Entering this text in a Search text box would find all Web pages that include **either** of the phrases.

Restricting Queries with the AND NOT Operator

If you use AND NOT in your search, the keyword or phrase that follows AND NOT will *not* appear on any of the Web pages returned by the search. AND NOT narrows your search so that you find fewer pages than if you hadn't used it. Use the AND NOT operator if your initial search returns too many irrelevant or unhelpful results, especially if you can think of a word or a phrase that a Web page shouldn't contain. Table B-3 gives you information about when to use AND NOT in your query. ✏ When you last searched for solar energy associations in Portland, you found too many Web pages about Portland, Maine, not Portland, Oregon. You want to find out if using AND NOT will eliminate those pages from your search results.

Steps

1. At the MSN Search site, click the **Advanced Search tab**, delete your previous query from the Search text box, type **"solar energy association" AND Portland**, then click the **Search button**

   After a few moments, your search results appear. They include Web pages about both cities—Portland, Oregon and Portland, Maine. A diagram of your search is shown in Figure B-12.

2. Use the Project File to record how many Web pages this search found

   You want to use AND NOT to exclude Web pages about Portland, Maine.

3. Click the **Advanced Search tab**, delete your previous query from the Search text box, type **"solar energy association" AND Portland AND NOT Maine**, then click the **Search button**

   A diagram of your search is shown in Figure B-13. The MSN search results appear as shown in Figure B-14. Note that this search made the set of search results smaller.

4. Use the Project File to record how many Web pages this search found, then answer the question for this lesson

   You have successfully limited your search to include Web pages that contain the phrase "*solar energy association*" and the keyword *Portland*, but not the word *Maine*.

TABLE B-3: The AND NOT operator

when to use AND NOT	variation of AND NOT at some search engines	advanced searching and AND NOT	search phrase and results
• To exclude undesirable words or phrases • To make your search more specific • When you are finding too many irrelevant results	• NOT • not (lowercase) • - (minus sign) • BUT NOT	Some search engines allow AND NOT searching at their advanced search pages. They may have pull-down menus or check boxes with words like: • Without the words • Must not contain • Must not include	"wind turbines" AND NOT Denmark Entering this text in a Search text box would find all Web pages that include the phrase "*wind turbines*" but **exclude** the word Denmark.

FIGURE B-12: Diagram of "solar energy association" AND Portland search

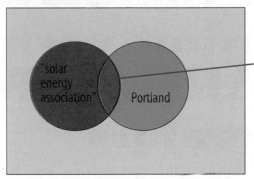

Web pages that contain **both** the phrase *"solar energy association" AND Portland* (the intersection of these two sets)

FIGURE B-13: Diagram of "solar energy association" AND Portland AND NOT Maine search

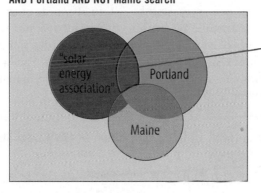

Web pages that contain **both** the phrase *"solar energy association"* and the word *Portland*, **but not** the word *Maine*

FIGURE B-14: MSN Advanced "solar energy association" AND Portland AND NOT Maine search

Search text box

Number of search results

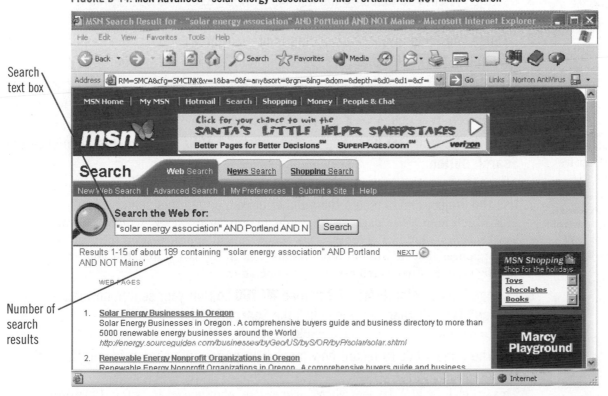

Searching by Proximity with NEAR/ and W/ Operators

In most cases, when you type two keywords in a Search text box, the search engine looks for the two words anywhere on a Web page, even hundreds of words apart and in any order. **Proximity operators** allow you to limit the distance between specific words on a Web page. Searching with the operator **NEAR/ 3** between two words means they must appear within 3 words of each other, although they may appear in any order. Using the **NEAR/ 50** operator means that the two words or phrases you enter must be within 50 words of each other on a Web page. If the order of the words matters, the **W/** (within) proximity operator will find the words within a specified number of words of each other, and only in the order you specify. For example, *war W/ 2 peace* will find *War and Peace*, not *Peace and War*. You have been looking for places that supply materials for solar energy. So far you have found too many, and you hope a proximity search will improve your search results.

Steps

Trouble?

If an advertisement window appears on top of the AOL window, click its Close button.

1. Go to the Student Online Companion at **www.course.com/illustrated/research**, then click **AOL Search**

   You are now ready to narrow your search for *solar energy supplies*.

2. Type **solar energy supplies** in the Search text box, then click the **Search button**

   Your search results appear, as shown in Figure B-15.

Trouble?

Can't find the number of search results at the top of the page? Try looking at the bottom, right-hand side.

3. Use the Project File to record the number of Web pages this search found

   A large number of Web pages have these three words somewhere on them.

4. Change your search query by adding quotation marks around the search terms so they appear as **"solar energy supplies"**, then click the **Search button**

5. Use the Project File to record the number of search results

   Searching for the phrase *"solar energy supplies"* was very restrictive and found too few results. Try a proximity search to see if you can find a more optimal number of results.

QuickTip

Insert a space between the slash (/) and the number.

6. Click the **Search text box**, type **"solar energy" NEAR/ 100 supplies**, then click the **Search button**

   After a few moments, your search results appear as shown in Figure B-16.

QuickTip

The NEAR/ operator does not need a number after it. At AOL Search the NEAR command will default to finding the two words within one word of each other.

7. Use the Project File to record the number of Web pages this search found

   This search found Web pages that have the phrase *"solar energy"* within 100 words of the word *supplies*—and in any order; *"solar energy"* might appear first on the page, or *supplies* might appear first. You found more results than in the last search, but you want to try a slightly more focused search using the W/ operator.

8. Change the operator **NEAR/ 100** to read **W/ 100** so that your search now reads **"solar energy" W/ 100 supplies**, then click the **Search button**

   After a few moments, your search results appear.

9. Use the Project File to record how many Web pages this search found, then answer the question for this lesson

   This search located Web pages where *"solar energy"* and *supplies* are within 100 words of each other, but *supplies* appears only after *"solar energy"*, not before it.

FIGURE B-15: AOL solar energy supplies search

Search text box

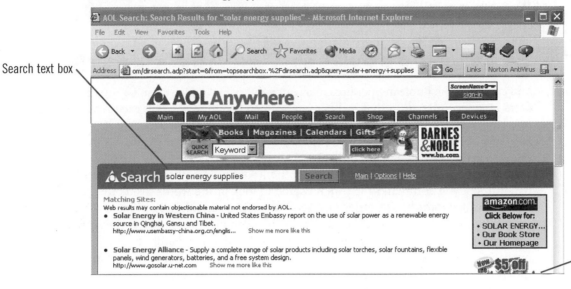

Number of search results at bottom of page

FIGURE B-16: AOL "solar energy" NEAR/ 100 supplies search

Search text box

Number of search results at bottom of page

CLUES TO USE

When to use NEAR/ or W/

Think of how the keywords or phrases you are searching for might appear on a Web page. In English, words often can appear before or after each other and still make sense. In the example in this lesson, a desired Web page might contain a phrase like "... supplies for solar energy and..." or "...our solar energy and wind power supplies are the best in...." Since either order works in English, it makes sense to consider using the NEAR/ operator.

Sometimes only one particular word order makes sense, like "wind turbines" or "wind powered turbines." After all, you'd never expect a relevant Web page to have the phrases "turbines wind" or "turbines wind powered" on it. Since only one order makes sense, use the W/ operator—wind W/ 2 turbines.

Combining Operators for Power Searches

You can combine Boolean operators in a search query for optimal results. You can use any operators in any combination that makes sense. Remember, however, that each AND or AND NOT operator added to your search narrows it, while each OR operator broadens it. When using more than one operator in a search query, you may need to use parentheses around groups of words to make sure the search engine translates your search correctly. A search engine usually reads your query from left to right, and so will apply the Boolean operators in that order. When you use parentheses, you command the search engine to look at the words inside the parentheses first, which is called **forcing the order of operation**. Using parentheses can make a big difference in your search results. An example of the results of a complex search where the search engine read the query from left to right is shown in Figure B-17. Forcing the order of operation of the search by using parentheses gives a better set of results, as shown in Figure B-18. ➤ You want to find information about thermal energy and geothermal power near you in Portland, Oregon. You decide to combine Boolean operators in a power search.

Steps

1. Go to the Student Online Companion at **www.course.com/illustrated/research**, then click the **MSN Search link**

   You are now ready to try your initial search.

2. Click the **Advanced Search tab**, type **thermal OR geothermal** in the Search text box, then click the **Search button**

   After a few moments, your search results appear.

3. Use the Project File to record how many Web pages this search found

   You need to limit your results to Web pages that specifically refer to *thermal or geothermal power or energy*.

4. Click the **Advanced Search tab**, delete your previous query in the Search text box, type **(thermal OR geothermal) AND (power OR energy)**, then click the **Search button**

   After a few moments, your search results appear.

5. Use the Project File to record how many Web pages this search found

   The number of search results is still unwieldy. You need to limit your search to find pages relating to Portland, Oregon.

6. Click the **Advanced Search tab**, edit your search to read **(thermal OR geothermal) AND (power OR energy) AND "Portland Oregon"** in the Search text box, then click the **Search button**

   Your search results appear.

7. Use the Project File to record the number of search results, then answer the question for this lesson

   By combining Boolean operators, this power search found a more manageable set of relevant search results.

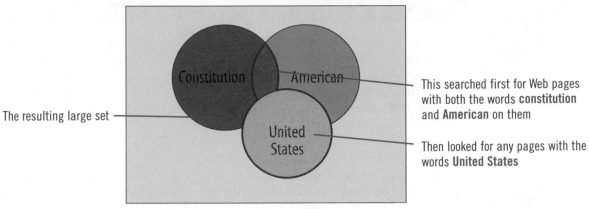

The resulting large set

This searched first for Web pages with both the words **constitution** and **American** on them

Then looked for any pages with the words **United States**

FIGURE B-18: Diagram of Constitution AND (American OR United States) search

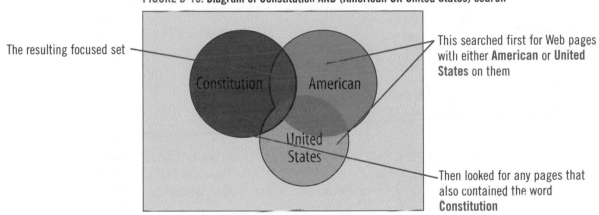

The resulting focused set

This searched first for Web pages with either **American** or **United States** on them

Then looked for any pages that also contained the word **Constitution**

CLUES TO USE

Setting up a power search

Developing an effective power search is easy. If you were looking for information about General Electric's plans to take over a rival company in France, you could follow these steps:

step	example
1. Isolate the first group of synonyms, or near synonyms, from your topic and link them with the Boolean OR.	General Electric **OR** GE
2. Add parentheses around this group of synonyms.	(General Electric **OR** GE)
3. Isolate the second group of synonyms and link them with the Boolean OR.	takeover **OR** expansion
4. Add parentheses around this group of synonyms.	(takeover **OR** expansion)
5. Do the same with any other groups of synonyms that you have.	
6. Now link all of the parenthetical groups (or single keywords or phrases) together with the Boolean **AND**.	(General Electric OR GE) **AND** (takeover OR expansion) **AND** France

Internet Research

Internet Research

Searching with Filters

Another great way to refine and focus a search is by using filters. **Filters** are programs that search engines use to screen out Web pages and other files on the World Wide Web. They are usually located at a search engine's Advanced Search page. Before you type your search query, you can choose filters to block out large areas of the Web from your search. For example, you can use language filters to search only for Web pages written in English, or you can use date filters to search only for Web pages updated in the last year. Filters are often activated by choosing from a pull-down menu or by typing special filter command words in the Search text box, examples of which are shown in Table B-4. Different Web file types like images, audio, or video can also be filter choices at search engines. A colleague in your office told you that Denmark is a leader in wind power. You want to locate wind power sites from Denmark, but since your Danish is a bit rusty, you need to find only Web pages in English. You will use filters to focus your search.

1. Go to the Student Online Companion at **www.course.com/illustrated/research**, click the **Google Search link**, then click **Advanced Search** (to the right of the Search text box)
The Google Advanced Search page appears.

2. Click the **Language filter pull-down menu**, then choose **English**
English should be selected, as in Figure B-19. Using this filter, you will only find Web pages written in English. Now you want to restrict your search to the domain exclusive to Denmark, which appears as *dk* in the URL.

3. Type **.dk** in the Domains filter text box
The Domains text box should appear as in Figure B-19. Using this filter you will only find Web pages in Denmark. (For more on Domains, see "The parts of a URL" Clues box.)

4. Type **wind power** in the Exact phrase text box, then click the **Google Search button**
Your search results should resemble those shown in Figure B-20. The Web pages in the set of results should contain the phrase *wind power*, should be written in English, and should be located in the Denmark domain.

5. Use the Project File to record some of the things you notice about the Search results page
For example, look in the Search text box on your results page, or at Figure B-20. Google has translated your search as "*wind power*" *site:.dk*. The *site:.dk* is how Google translated your choice of .*dk* in the Domains filter. Look also just below the tabs at the top left of the search results page. Google reiterated your search query as Searched *English* pages for "*wind power*" *site:.dk*. This information provides a good way to determine whether the filters worked the way you thought they would when you set up your search.

6. Save, print, and close the Project File

TABLE B-4: Examples of filters available at Google

Text box or pull-down menu filters	**Language** limits your search to sites written in the language you choose. **Date** limits your search to Web pages updated within a specified time period. **Domains** limits your search to words found at a certain domain name or type (.edu, .com, etc.). **SafeSearch** limits your search to child-friendly sites.
Command word filters (used in the regular search text box)	**inurl** limits your search to words found directly in the URL. **intitle** limits your search to words found in the title of a Web page. **site** limits your search to words found at a certain domain name or type (.edu, .com, etc.). **link** finds only Web pages linked to a specified URL.

FIGURE B-19: Google filtered search set-up

Boolean AND search

Boolean phrase search

Boolean OR search

Boolean AND NOT search

Filters

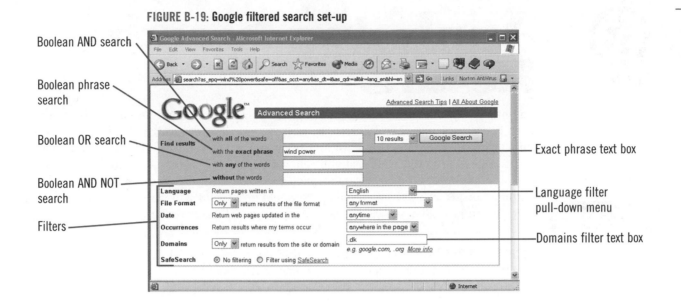

Exact phrase text box

Language filter pull-down menu

Domains filter text box

FIGURE B-20: Google filtered search results

Google search translation

Search reiteration

Text in English

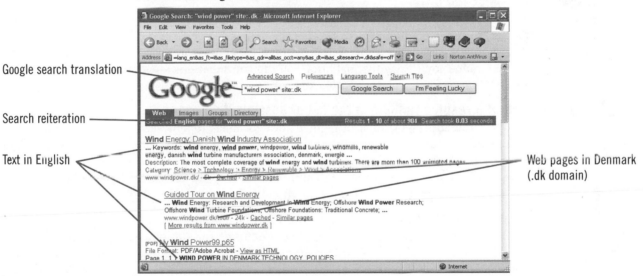

Web pages in Denmark (.dk domain)

CLUES TO USE

The parts of a URL

Filters, such as Domains and site, search only for words that appear in parts of a URL. The URL www.wind.dk/english/home.html, for example, has the following parts:

www.wind.dk /english /home .html
domain *directory* *page* *file extension*

For Web sites in the United States, the last part of a domain name can be three letters that represent the type of organization hosting the Web site. University domains often end in .edu; government sites end in .gov; commercial sites end in .com; and non-profits end in .org. Web sites located in other countries use two-letter country codes, like .fr for France, .uk for the United Kingdom, and .de for Germany (Deutschland). Any of these two- or three-letter codes can be used to limit search results when using filters. For a full listing of the two-letter country codes, go to www.iana.org/cctld/cctld-whois.htm.

Analyzing Search Results

Up until now you have been concentrating on finding the optimal number of search results by using Boolean operators and filters. The next step is to scan the search results pages in order to quickly find the Web sites that seem to match most closely your search query. A search engine's results page offers many clues that will help you zero in on your target. Knowing how to read a page of search results and navigate through them can save you time. ✏️ You realize that learning how to scan a search results page would be a useful skill. You decide to look closely at a search you just did at www.google.com on *geothermal energy resources*.

Details

▶ **Locate your search terms within the search result**

Search engines often display snippets of text that contain your keywords. The number of times your keywords show up in the snippet may indicate the relevance of the Web page to your search. The proximity of the words may also indicate relevance, as would a keyword in the URL. In the example in Figure B-21 (the results for the search *geothermal energy resources*), Google has highlighted your search terms for easy scanning. The word *geothermal* appears four times and the exact phrase *geothermal energy resources* appears once. *Geothermal* is also part of the URL—www.**geothermal**.org.

▶ **Decipher the URL**

The name of a URL is often **mnemonic;** that is, it indicates what the Web site is about so that its URL is easier to remember. The end of the domain name (.com, .edu, .fr, .jp, etc.) also indicates either a certain type of Web site or its geographic domain. In the second example, www.eren.doe.gov/RE/geothermal.html, you can guess that this is a **gov**ernmental site from the **D**epartment **o**f **E**nergy about **geothermal** matters.

▶ **Note the result's ranking in the list of possible Web pages**

Search engines use **algorithms**, or mathematical formulas, to rank each Web site according to the terms used in your search query. Every search engine has a slightly different algorithm for figuring out the "best," but all of them put their best picks first in a list. Generally speaking, you shouldn't have to go through more than three or four pages of search results to find the pages you want. If you do, try refining your search.

▶ **Determine if the search engine uses directory links**

More and more search engines are creating **directories** (or **subject guides**) of recommended Web sites on many subjects. If a search engine site has taken the time to include a Web page in its directory, it often may indicate relevance. Note the Google directory links in Figure B-21. Clicking a directory link sends you directly to Google's list of Web pages related to geothermal issues.

▶ **Determine if the search engine uses cached pages**

Sometimes links to Web pages break. Search engines may not become aware of the problem until their spiders search that part of the Web again. As a result, when you click a link you may get a computer error message instead. Google has hidden, or **cached**, copies of the Web pages found at their site. If you click the word Cached, you will see the older copy of the Web page with the keywords highlighted, as shown in Figure B-22. Cached pages can sometimes help you find the newer or renamed version of the page, or find authors' names or other specific terms. Try a new search query using those terms.

▶ **Navigate between search results pages**

Search results are usually displayed 10 or 20 to a page. In large searches there may be hundreds of pages of search results. At Google you need to go to the bottom of a search result page in order to navigate to a different page, as shown in Figure B-23.

FIGURE B-21: Google search results page

Preferences let you customize results display

Keywords in page title and snippets

URL

Directory or subject guide link

Cached page

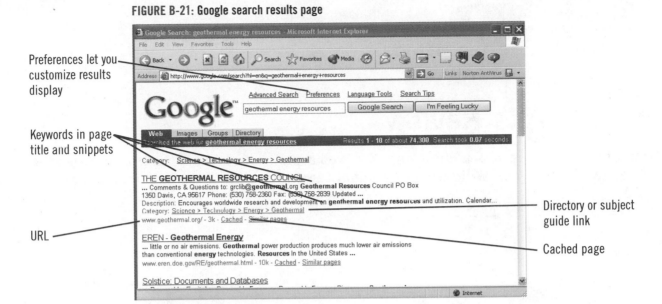

FIGURE B-22: Google cache of the Geothermal Resources Council's page

Note that this is a cached page

Highlighted keywords

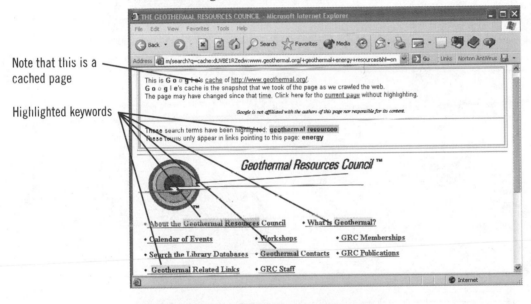

FIGURE B-23: Bottom of Google search results page

Other search results pages

Next page option

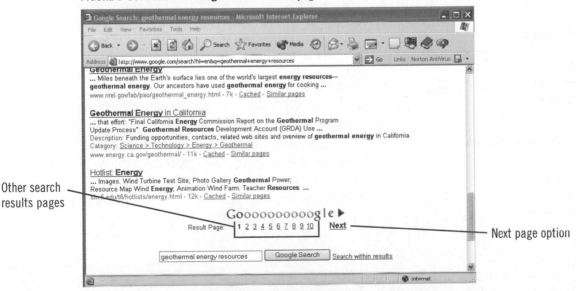

Practice

► Concepts Review

Each of the following sets is the result of a Web search where the rectangle indicates the entire World Wide Web. Write down the initial search for each of the sets indicated.

FIGURE B-24

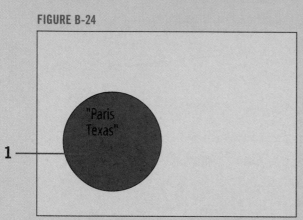

1

FIGURE B-25

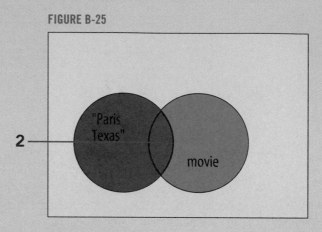

2

FIGURE B-26

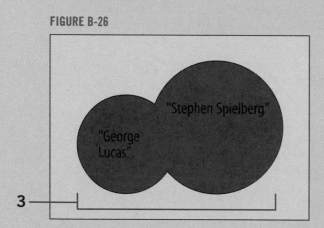

3

FIGURE B-27

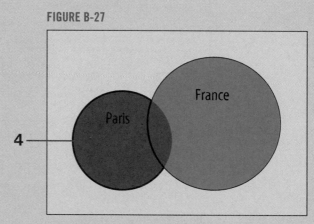

4

Match each of the following terms with the statement that best describes it:

5. Boolean operators
6. Venn diagrams
7. The AND operator
8. The OR Operator
9. The AND NOT operator
10. The W/ operator
11. Parentheses
12. Filters
13. An algorithm

a. A way to visualize how Boolean operators work.
b. Is used to connect synonyms.
c. A mathematical formula used by search engines to rank search results.
d. Aids to screen out unwanted Web pages.
e. Force the order of operation in a Boolean search.
f. Is used to exclude words from a search query.
g. A way to narrow a search.
h. Indicate how keywords are to relate to each other in a search query.
i. Is an example of a proximity operator.

14. The place where two search result sets overlap is called the _____ of the two sets.
    a. Union
    b. Combination
    c. Intersection
    d. Margin

15. Each time you use the Boolean operator AND to link one keyword to another, you will find:
    a. More and more Web pages.
    b. Exactly the same number of Web pages.
    c. Fewer and fewer Web pages.
    d. None of the above.

16. The equivalent wording for the Boolean OR in a pull-down menu might be:
    a. Either of the words.
    b. All of the words.
    c. None of the words.
    d. Must not contain.

17. Which is **NOT** a variation of the Boolean operator AND NOT?
    a. NOT
    b. - (the minus sign)
    c. NOT MORE
    d. BUT NOT

18. Both NEAR/ and W/:
    a. Are proximity operators.
    b. Find words close to each other and in any order.
    c. Find words only within 25 words of each other.
    d. Are approximate operators.

19. If you do **NOT** force the order of operation in a complex Boolean search, the search engine will:
    a. Read the query from left to right.
    b. Insert the parentheses for you.
    c. Return no search results.
    d. Automatically apply filters to your search.

20. There are _____ spaces in a URL.
    a. Never
    b. Always
    c. Often
    d. Sometimes

21. The part of a URL that can contain a two-letter country code is the:
    a. File.
    b. File extension.
    c. Domain.
    d. Page.

22. The names of URLs tend to be _____ so that you can remember them better.
- **a.** Algorithmic
- **b.** Boolean
- **c.** Proximate
- **d.** Mnemonic

23. Which is something you would NOT usually do when analyzing your search results?
- **a.** Locate your search terms within the search result.
- **b.** Go directly to the fourth page of search results.
- **c.** Attempt to decipher the URL.
- **d.** Customize how your search results are displayed.

 Skills Review

1. Understand Boolean operators.
- **a.** In a word processor or text editor, open the file called **SR-B.rtf** and save it as **IR Skills Review-B.rtf**.
- **b.** Use this file to explain three uses of Boolean operators.
- **c.** Add your name to the top of the page.

2. Narrow a search with the AND operator.
- **a.** Open your browser and go to the Student Online Companion at www.course.com/illustrated/research, then click the MSN Search engine link.
- **b.** Click the Advanced Search tab, then perform the initial search **"lunar landing"** to find information about proposed Chinese lunar landings.
- **c.** Use the Project File to record the number of search results.
- **d.** Return to the Advanced Search page.
- **e.** Perform the search query **"lunar landing" AND China**.
- **f.** Use the Project File to record the number of search results, then answer the question.

3. Expand a Search with the OR operator.
- **a.** Go to the Student Online Companion at www.course.com/illustrated/research, then click the MSN Search engine link.
- **b.** Click the Advanced Search tab, then perform the initial search **"cat distemper"** to find information about whether your cat needs a cat distemper shot (you don't know if the shot is called cat distemper or feline distemper).
- **c.** Use the Project File to record the number of search results.
- **d.** Return to the Advanced Search page.
- **e.** Now perform the search query **"cat distemper" OR "feline distemper"**.
- **f.** Use the Project File to record the number of search results, then answer the question.

4. Restrict a Search with the AND NOT operator
- **a.** Go to the Student Online Companion at www.course.com/illustrated/research, then click the MSN Search engine link.
- **b.** Click the Advanced Search tab, then perform the initial search **"vampire bat"**.
- **c.** Use the Project File to record the number of search results.
- **d.** Return to the Advanced Search page.
- **e.** Now perform the search query **"vampire bat" AND NOT Dracula**.
- **f.** Use the Project File to record the number of search results, then answer the question.

5. **Search by proximity with NEAR/ and W/ operators.**
   a. Go to the Student Online Companion at www.course.com/illustrated/research, then click the AOL Search link.
   b. Perform the initial search **Roosevelt W/ 25 "New Deal"**.
   c. Use the Project File to record the number of search results.
   d. Now perform the search query **Roosevelt NEAR/ 25 "New Deal"**.
   e. Use the Project File to record the number of search results, then answer the question.

6. **Perform a power search.**
   a. Go to the Student Online Companion at www.course.com/illustrated/research, then click the MSN Search engine link.
   b. Click the Advanced Search tab, then perform the complex search **(Michelangelo OR Brunelleschi) AND Duomo AND Florence** (in order to determine whether Michelangelo or Brunelleschi created the Duomo in Florence, Italy).
   c. Use the Project File to record the number of search results, then answer the question.

7. **Search with filters.**
   a. Go to the Student Online Companion at www.course.com/illustrated/research, then click the Google Search engine link.
   b. Click Advanced Search.
   c. In the Exact phrase text box, type the search **Chinese New Year**.
   d. Choose English from the Language filter pull-down menu.
   e. In the Domains text box, type **.edu** so that the search results include only academic information.
   f. Click the Google Search button.
   g. Use the Project File to answer the question about this step.

8. **Analyze search results.**
   a. Use the Project File to answer the questions about how to analyze search results.
   b. Save, print, and close the Project File.

Independent Challenge 1

You want to find Web sites in Russia (domain .ru) about the Hermitage Museum. You don't read Russian so you want the Web pages to be in English.

a. Use the Student Online Companion (www.course.com/illustrated/research) to go to the Google Advanced Search page.

b. Set the appropriate filters and perform your search.

c. Print out the first page of Search results.

d. Add your name to the top of the printout.

 # Independent Challenge 2

You want to explain to a friend how Boolean operators work. You decide to draw a series of three Venn diagrams to illustrate what happens when you use AND, OR, and AND NOT in a search.

a. Draw a Venn diagram that represents how the AND operator works and label it "The AND operator."

b. Draw a Venn diagram that represents how the OR operator works and label it "The OR operator."

c. Draw a Venn diagram that represents how the AND NOT operator works and label it "The AND NOT operator."

d. Add your name to the top of the page(s).

 # Independent Challenge 3

Your history teacher has told you that there is a connection between the Library of Congress and Thomas Jefferson. You decide to search the Internet to find out what the connection is.

a. Write down the two key phrases in this search.

b. Put quotes around each of the separate phrases.

c. Combine the phrases with either the NEAR/ 50 operator or the W/ 50 operator. (Your search should have the form *"first phrase" NEAR/ 50 "second phrase"* or *"first phrase" W/ 50 "second phrase".*)

d. Open your browser and use the Student Online Companion (www.course.com/illustrated/research) to go to AOL Search and perform this search.

e. Print the first page of search results.

f. Put your name on the top of the printout.

Independent Challenge 4

You and some friends want to go scuba diving or snorkeling in either Costa Rica or Panama. You are particularly interested in an ecotour.

   a. Write the topic on a sheet of paper and circle the key phrases. *Hint:* You should find two phrases and three keywords.

   b. Write each two-word phrase or keyword on a separate line.

   c. Surround each of the phrases in quotes.

   d. Start your search query by combining the synonyms together with the Boolean operator OR, then surround these synonyms with parentheses. *Hint:* There are two sets of synonyms. Your search should have the form *("first phrase" OR keyword)*.

   e. Continue developing the search query by linking the phrases, and other keywords, together with AND.

   f. Write down the completed search query. It should have the form *("first phrase" OR keyword) AND ("second phrase" OR keyword) AND keyword*.

   g. Open your browser and use the Student Online Companion (www.course.com/illustrated/research) to go to MSN Advanced Search and perform the search.

   h. Print out a copy of the first page of your search results.

   i. Attach the printout to the paper that has your topic and key phrases written on it.

   j. Add your name to the top of the page.

 # Independent Challenge 5

You want to find information about the Peloponnesian War.

   a. Open your browser and go to a search engine.

   b. Perform a search and print out the first page of search results.

   c. Analyze the search results. Judging only from the information on the search results page, decide which link you think would contain the best information about the Peloponnesian War.

   d. Circle the link that you think is the best.

   e. Use a word processor or pen and paper to record the reasons you chose that link as the best one.

   f. Add your name to the top of the paper, and attach your printout to it.

▶ Visual Workshop

A friend of yours knows of your interest in bonsai and happened upon a Web page that she thought you might find interesting. She gave you a printout of the Web page (see Figure B-28). Unfortunately, the URL is not on that printout, and your friend can't remember how she found it.

a. Look at the Web page and choose some keywords that you might use to find this page. Write them down.

b. On the same page, construct a search query that you think will find this Web page.

c. Go to an Internet Search engine and perform your search. (You may have to adjust your search as you go.)

d. Once you find this Web page, print out a copy, and attach it to the paper on which you've written your query. (*Note*: If this page no longer exists on the Web, find one on the same subject.)

e. Add your name to the top of your paper.

FIGURE B-28

Japanese Maple 'Sangokaku'
(*Acer palmatum*)

The Bonsai Site...

Description : The Japanese maple is the most widely grown maple in gardens and is a perfect subject for bonsai. It is valued for its compact size, delicate ferny foliage and brilliant fall (autumn) colouring - from rich gold to deepest blood-red. Although more tolerant of winter climates than most maples, it needs shade and shelter or leaves may shrivel. The more than 300 cultivars range from rock garden miniatures to vigorous small trees, with a variety of leaf shape, size and colour. *'Sangokaku'* (syn. *'Senkaki'*) has coral branches and twigs, which are bare in winter - producing a wonderful show.

Age : Created in 1990

Main Page
Introduction
History
Styles
Advanced Techniques
Gallery
Additional Features
Maintenance
Plant Profiles
Survey
Bonsai Books
Bonsai Seeds
Forum
FAQ
Join Our Newsletter
Site Map -
Link To Us -

Browsing

Subject Guides

Objectives

- ► **Understand subject guides**
- ► **Browse a subject guide**
- ► **Search a subject guide**
- ► **Navigate a subject guide**
- ► **Tap trailblazer pages**
- ► **Use specialized search engines**
- ► **Understand evaluative criteria**
- ► **Evaluate Web pages**

You have seen how a simple search of the World Wide Web can yield thousands, or even millions, of Web pages. Filtering through those Web pages on your own can be a daunting task. However, subject guides can help you focus your search to find the information you want. A **subject guide** groups information on the Internet by topic, usually alphabetically. These topics let you quickly acquaint yourself with the breadth and/or depth of a particular subject. You can navigate or browse a subject guide in a variety ways, including "drilling-down" through a set of hierarchical links or searching the subject guide using a query statement. While subject guides are typically compiled by subject-matter experts rather than by a software program, you still need to know how to evaluate the information a subject guide helps you find. To gather general information about alternative energy, as well as learn what experts in the field think are important sources of information, you decide to investigate some authoritative subject guides.

Understanding Subject Guides

Subject guides bring order to the chaos of the Internet and the World Wide Web. The people who create subject guides are like librarians: They are selective, and try to compile only the best resources. They also arrange links together topically for easy access. Some subject guides cover many areas, while others select academic information; some catalog resources for K-12 students, and others select only sources applicable to higher education. Subject guides are also known as subject directories, Internet directories, and subject trees. See Table C-1 for information about subject guides. ✒ In order to become a more efficient user of the Internet, you decide to learn more about subject guides so that you can use them to your advantage.

Details

► ## Organization

Subject guides are organized by topic in a hierarchical fashion. A **hierarchy** is a ranked order. Subject guides usually start with a list of general topics. For example, the general topics shown in boldface type in the Librarians' Index to the Internet subject guide shown in Figure C-1 are followed by lists of related, more specific topics (shown in normal type). Clicking a topic such as "Science" will link you to a list of sub-topics. Sub-topics will often link you to yet another level of more detailed topics.

► ## Selectivity and small size

Subject guides are selective by definition. More important, *people*, rather than the computer programs run by search engines, decide which Web pages are worthy of inclusion in a subject guide. They often include **trailblazer pages**, or Web pages that link to other sites that cover all aspects of a topic. Subject experts also include sites that might cover one or two very detailed sub-topics. This kind of selectivity ensures that the Web pages returned by your search are some of the best on the subject. Because of their specialization, as well as the careful selection process, subject guides are relatively small compared to the size of the World Wide Web. This smaller size is actually one of a subject guide's strengths, as it saves you the time and trouble of sifting through thousands of search engine results.

► ## Annotations

The annotations provided by subject guides for each Web page listed also make subject guides the tools of choice for many researchers. **Annotations** are carefully written summaries or reviews of the contents of a Web page, an example of which is shown in Figure C-2. The experts who create a subject guide also write its annotations. These annotations are great time-savers, as they allow you to preview a site before going to it. In this way, you can eliminate unhelpful sites without a lot of review work on your part.

► ## Access methods

Besides the hierarchical list of topics, subject guides usually provide other methods to access the Web pages they list. A local search engine usually allows you to search either the titles of the Web pages or the annotations. A subject guide might also provide a list of topics arranged alphabetically, or organized using the Dewey Decimal system.

► ## Results display

Subject guides display results differently than search engines do. A typical display of results is shown in Figure C-2. The directory displays the number of results for your topic at the top of the page. At the bottom is a list of other subject terms under which this site is indexed. By clicking any of these links, you can go to similarly indexed sites. Figure C-2 uses the Librarians' Index to the Internet as its example, but other subject guides are organized in a similar fashion.

FIGURE C-1: General topics at Librarians' Index to the Internet

General topics (bold type)

Sub-topics (regular type)

Link to alphabetical list of topics

Science link

FIGURE C-2: Example of subject guide Web site display

The topic you selected

Title of Web site

Annotation

Other subjects under which this site is indexed

Number of Web sites on this topic

Web site URL

Reviewers' initials and dates reviewed

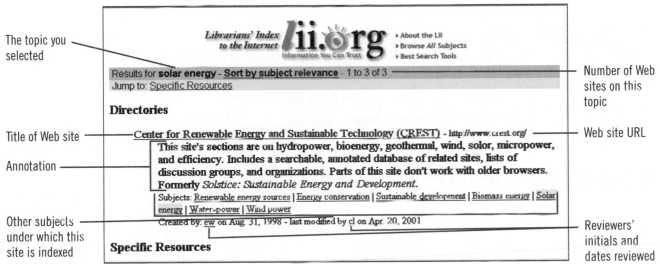

TABLE C-1: Special features of select subject guides (see the Student Online Companion at www.course.com/illustrated/research)

name	scope/level	size (pages indexed)	special features
About.com	General	1 million+	Very broad and surprisingly deep at times, this guide provides chat rooms and featured articles.
BUBL LINK 5:15	Academic subject areas	11,000+	Aims to provide between 5 and 15 sources for each subject.
INFOMINE	University level research sites	22,000+	Links to electronic journals, databases, and conference proceedings.
Librarians' Index to the Internet	Public library level	8,500	Sites selected and evaluated by librarians.
LookSmart	Popular/commercial	2.5 million	Leans heavily toward commercial sites.
Open Directory	General/all encompassing	3 million	Many search tools use this free service. Maintained by volunteer editors. Uneven coverage.
Virtual Library	General/all encompassing	?	Volunteers maintain this distributed guide, the oldest catalog of the Web.

Browsing a Subject Guide

Internet Research

Browsing is the easiest and most effective way to find information in a subject guide. The creators of the subject guide have reviewed the Web sites and organized them by topic. By clicking your way through the hierarchy of topics, from the most general to the most specific, you can quickly arrive at what the guide's creators deem to be the best Web sites on most any subject. You decide to continue your search for information about alternative energy by browsing a few subject guides.

Steps

1. Open the Project File **IR-C1.rtf** in your word processing program (from the drive and folder where your Project Files are stored), save it as **Subject Guides.rtf**, open your browser, go to the Student Online Companion at **www.course.com/illustrated/research**, then click the **Librarians' Index link** (under "Subject guides")

    The Librarians' Index to the Internet (LII) home page should appear. Looking at all of the general topics available, you decide that your topic, "alternative energy," might be under "Science."

2. On the LII home page, click the word **Science**

    The sub-topics under "Science" appear as in Figure C-3. Again you have to make a choice. You decide that your topic will probably be under "Environment."

3. On the Science Topics page, click **Environment**

    The sub-topics under "Environment" appear. Many of them might be useful, including "Energy Conservation," "Environmental Responsibility," "Renewable Energy," "Solar Energy," "Sustainable Development," and "Wind Power." You decide to look at "Renewable Energy."

4. On the Environment Topics page, click **Renewable Energy**

    The Web sites related to renewable energy appear, as in Figure C-4. You have found the sites that LII deems most relevant to your search. Note that the sites at the top of the list are listed under the term "Directories," extensive Web sites that cover a large portion of the topic. The sites toward the bottom of the page, "Specific Resources," are very detailed, specialized sites. Now you want to look at a distributed subject guide to see what kind of information you can find there.

5. Go to the **Student Online Companion**, then click the **Virtual Library link** (under "Subject guides")

    Notice that the terms in the initial topic list appear somewhat academic. You decide to look for alternative energy sites under the topic "Engineering."

6. Click **Engineering**, then click **Chemical Engineering**

    This page is organized differently than the last few pages you viewed. The background color has changed, and looking at the domain name of the URL you see it is no longer vlib.org.

7. Scroll down the page, if necessary, then click **Energy, Conservation and Efficiency**

    You now see a list of relevant Web sites with short annotations.

8. On the Energy, Conservation, and Efficiency page, scroll through the list of Web sites, select an annotated site, answer the questions about "Scope" in the Project File, then save the Project File

    You notice that many of the Web sites listed relate to the topic of energy in general; there are even a few sites related to your topic of "alternative energy."

FIGURE C-3: Sub-topics under "Science"

Main topic heading

Sub-topics with further subdivisions (**bold type**)

"Environment" sub-topics link

Sub-topics with no further sub-divisions (regular type)

FIGURE C-4: Renewable energy Web sites

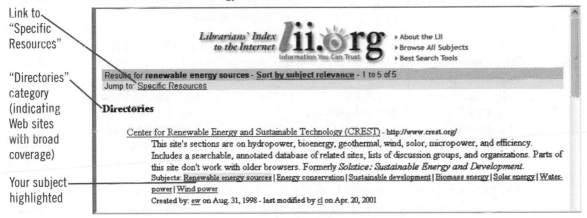

Link to "Specific Resources"

"Directories" category (indicating Web sites with broad coverage)

Your subject highlighted

CLUES TO USE

Understanding annotated and distributed subject guides

Most subject guides are **annotated**, and include summaries written by reviewers. Some subject guides, such as the Virtual Library or the Open Directory Project, are distributed subject guides. **Distributed subject guides** have been created by a variety of editors working somewhat independently. Each editor is usually responsible for a sub-topic of the main topic.

These guides are said to be "distributed" because the Web pages for each guide are stored (or "distributed") on different computers. Because distributed subject guides have many contributors, all with varying levels of expertise, they tend to have a somewhat uneven quality and may lack standardization.

Searching a Subject Guide

The hierarchical arrangements of topics that characterize subject guides are not always as useful as they should be. Different people maintain each subject guide, and everyone has his or her own way of organizing Web information. As you saw in the last lesson, "Energy" might appear under the general topic of "Science" at one guide, and under "Engineering" at another. For this reason, a more direct approach to finding information has been added to many subject guides—a local search engine. A subject guide search engine doesn't search the Web like the search engines you used in Units A and B. Instead, this kind of search engine searches *only* the titles of the Web pages and the annotations indexed at the subject guide site. This is a much smaller database than the whole Web, and you must adjust your search strategy accordingly. When searching a subject guide, try to use just one word or a two-word phrase. You can try very specific words like "photovoltaic" or "bioenergy," but if they don't work, you can try broader concepts like "solar power" or "renewable energy." You want to find more Web information about geothermal energy. You decide to use the LookSmart Subject Guide.

Steps

QuickTip

Looking at LookSmart, you'll see no real indication that you are searching a subject guide; in fact, it even erroneously invites you to "Search the Web." Read the "About" pages at the site if you are in doubt as to whether the Search tool you are using is a subject guide or a search engine.

1. Go to the **Student Online Companion at www.course.com/illustrated/research**, then click the **LookSmart link** (under "Subject guides")

The LookSmart home page should appear, as shown in Figure C-5. Since you are not sure which general topic to choose for a general Web search, you will try searching the LookSmart subject guide instead. Remember that subject guides usually index trailblazer Web sites, or sites that cover large subject areas. Because your search query consists of only one or two words, Boolean operators are not necessary, or even desirable.

2. In the Search text box, type **geothermal**, then click the **Search button**

Your search results should be similar to those shown in Figure C-6. Notice how these results are displayed. The first result is a "Featured Listing," meaning it's a Web site that has paid LookSmart to be placed at the top of the list. The next few lines are LookSmart "Directory Categories." **Directory Categories** are the topics that LookSmart has developed for the word "geothermal." At the bottom of the page, under "Reviewed Web Sites," are actual links (with annotations) to Web sites related to your topic. You decide to follow the directory category "Geothermal Energy."

3. Click the Directory Category **Geothermal Energy**

The Web page of results appears as in Figure C-7. Notice the "Featured Sponsors" links at the top of the page. Again, these are companies paying to advertise at LookSmart. In the middle of the page are the words "You are here" followed by a directory path Home > Work & Money > Industries > Energy & Utilities > Energy by Type > Geothermal. This is LookSmart's way of telling you where you are in their subject guide. If you started from the home page topics, you could click "Work & Money," then "Industries," then "Energy & Utilities" to get to "Geothermal." At the bottom of the screen are the recommended Web sites with short annotations.

Trouble?

In order to find the URL, sponsor and purpose of the site click the link to the site and hunt around. See if there is a Help or an About Us link on the page.

4. Look through the list of sites, read the annotations, then choose a site to answer the questions in the Project File relating to Objectivity

To determine the relative objectivity of the site, look to see who sponsors the site and what the stated purpose of the site is. Also look to see what kind of domain it is at (.com, .org, .edu, or .gov).

5. Save the Project File

FIGURE C-5: LookSmart subject guide

LookSmart subject guide Search the Web text box

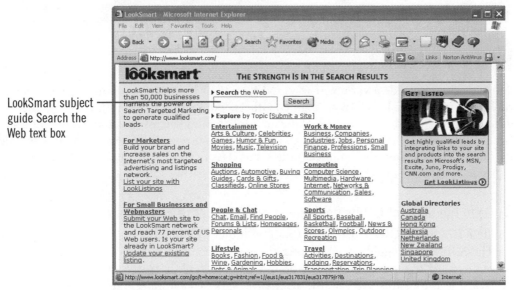

FIGURE C-6: Geothermal search at LookSmart

"Featured Listing"

LookSmart "Directory Categories"

Web sites with annotations

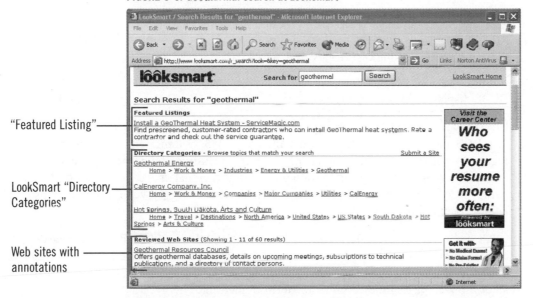

FIGURE C-7: Geothermal Energy "Directory Category" link results

"Featured Sponsors" advertiser's links

The directory path

Recommended Web sites

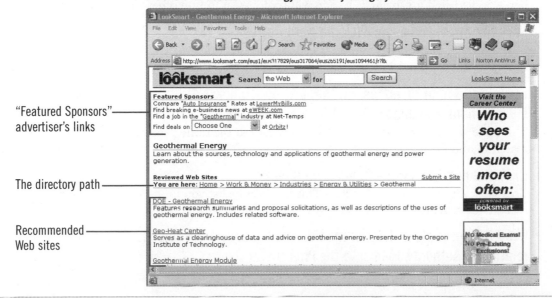

Internet Research

Navigating a Subject Guide

Subject guides provide a variety of ways to access their information. Some provide hierarchical lists of topics and local search engines. Others, like BUBL LINK / 5:15 (BUBL), offer many different ways to find what you're looking for. Alphabetical lists, as well as the usual topical subject menus, allow you to browse through the categories in a variety of ways. BUBL also indexes its site by **Dewey Decimal number**, the same classification system used in many libraries. You decide to explore alternative ways of navigating subject guides at BUBL.

1. Go to the Student Online Companion at **www.course.com/illustrated/research**, then click the **BUBL LINK / 5:15 link** (under "Subject guides")

   The BUBL subject guide should appear as shown in Figure C-8. Notice the usual general topics in the center of the page, and at the top and the bottom of the page a local subject guide search. Near the top of this page are the alternative ways of navigating through this subject guide: "Subject Menus," "A-Z," "Dewey," "Countries," and "Types." You decide to explore a few of them.

2. Click **Subject Menus** at the top of the BUBL page

   An alphabetical list of subjects appears. You decide to see if a subject in the list will help you in your alternative energy research.

3. Scroll down the page, then click **Energy**

   BUBL displays a list of sub-topics and their corresponding Dewey Decimal numbers.

QuickTip

You can use the descriptions at BUBL to help you determine the **authority** of a site. If you want further information about an author, search on his or her name. You can also use the Page last updated date to check for currency.

4. Click **333.79 Renewable energy**

   The Web sites indexed at BUBL under the term "333.79 Renewable energy" are shown in Figure C-9. BUBL provides useful information, including the author of each site. If the author is a group or organizaiton, rather than an individual, it is called a **corporate author**. Now that you know an appropriate term ("Renewable energy"), you decide to try using the alphabetical index.

5. Click **A-Z** at the top of the page, click the letter **R**, then click **Renewable energy**

   The list of Web sites related to renewable energy appears as shown in Figure C-10. BUBL displays the results two ways: On the left-hand side, for easy previewing, BUBL lists the titles of all of the Web pages indexed under the term "Renewable energy." To the right, BUBL lists the titles of the individual Web sites, as well as their annotations. You see the Dewey Class number 333.794 listed for the first site and will try to use it to find other similar ones.

6. Near the top of the page, click the word **Dewey**

   In the middle of the page, you see a list of the general Dewey Classification numbers, for example, 000, 100, and 200. You want to look for 333.794.

7. Click **300 Social sciences**, on the next page click **330 Economics**, then click **333 Environment and economics of land and energy**

   This page should look familiar. In fact, you reached the same page earlier using a different search method.

8. Click the number **333.79 Renewable energy**

   This page should look very familiar. This is the same list you found in Step 4 above. BUBL really does provide a lot of ways for you to access its information.

9. Read the description of one of the titles listed, answer the questions in the Project File relating to Authority, then save the Project File

FIGURE C-8: BUBL LINK 5:15

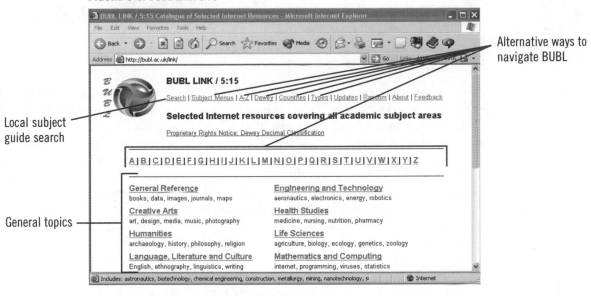

Alternative ways to navigate BUBL

Local subject guide search

General topics

FIGURE C-9: BUBL—"333.79 Renewable energy"

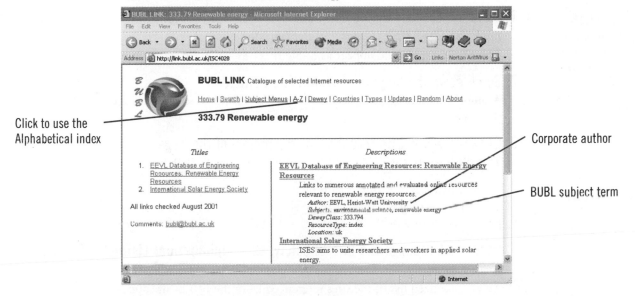

Click to use the Alphabetical index

Corporate author

BUBL subject term

FIGURE C-10: BUBL—Renewable Energy Web sites

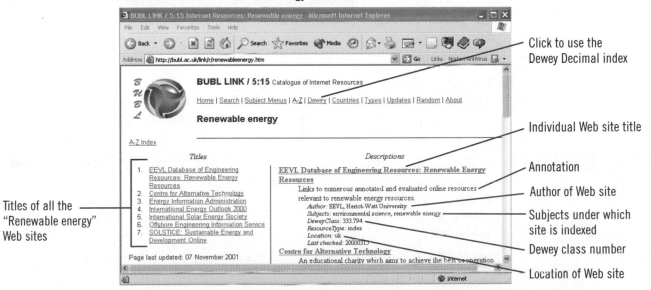

Click to use the Dewey Decimal index

Individual Web site title

Annotation

Author of Web site

Subjects under which site is indexed

Dewey class number

Location of Web site

Titles of all the "Renewable energy" Web sites

Tapping Trailblazer Pages

Many of the Web sites you have found using subject guides are called trailblazer pages. **Trailblazer pages** are created by scholars, experts, and organizations who want to provide links to all aspects of their subject. The scope of a trailblazer page may be narrow, like "photovoltaics," or broad, like "alternative energy," but all trailblazer pages have the same aim: they attempt to provide thorough coverage of their subject. A good trailblazer page will not only provide links to many useful Web sites, it will also provide a logical structure for presenting the links and an organized way of navigating them. Organizational features might include a search engine for the Web site itself, a **site map** (an index to the pages located at the site itself), and a consistent use of directional words and navigation buttons throughout the site. In order to maximize your use of trailblazer pages you need to familiarize yourself with the helpful structures they provide. A member of your alternative energy research team at City Hall has recommended the Department of Energy's *Energy Efficiency and Renewable Energy Network* site (EREN) as a gold-mine of information. You decide to take a few minutes exploring its organization.

Steps

Trouble?
Does the EREN Web site look different? Many Web sites change their looks over time. Usually the same information will still reside at the site; you may just have to click on slightly different links to find it.

1. Go to the Student Online Companion at **www.course.com/illustrated/research**, then click the **EREN link** (under "Subject guides")
   The EREN site should appear as in Figure C-11.

2. Scroll down the page to see how it's organized
   Along the left are links to various departments, and general topics are listed in the center of the page.

3. Click the words **Site Directory** at the bottom of the page
   This site links to over 600 other sites and contains over 80,000 documents at the EREN site itself.

4. Scroll down the Site Directory page
   This site directory is a map of the Web pages at the EREN site. You want to see a more comprehensive listing of the Web sites that EREN links to.

5. Near the bottom of the Site Directory, click **Alphabetical Listing of Sites** under the Search heading
   An alphabetized list of the sites referenced from the EREN site appears.

6. Scroll through the list, noticing how thorough it seems, scroll back to the top of the Alphabetical Listing of Sites page, then click the word **HOME** on the right-hand side of the page title
   The EREN home page reappears. You want to see how well the sub-topics are organized.

7. Click **Bioenergy** under Renewable Energy
   EREN's Web page for bioenergy should appear as in Figure C-12. Notice that along the left-hand side is an EREN Search text box as well as other links. You want to see if there is any information about your town, Portland, Oregon.

QuickTip
Whenever you find a great site like EREN, make sure to save it for further reference as an Internet Explorer Favorite or a Netscape Bookmark.

8. **Scroll** up to the top of the page (if necessary), type the phrase **"Portland Oregon"** in the Search text box, then click the **Search button**
   The EREN search results appear, as shown in Figure C-13. Notice the number of search results at the top of the page. After your thorough tour you've determined the EREN site is a goldmine.

9. Click the **Back button** 2 times, answer the question about Organization in the Project File, then save the file

FIGURE C-11: EREN home page

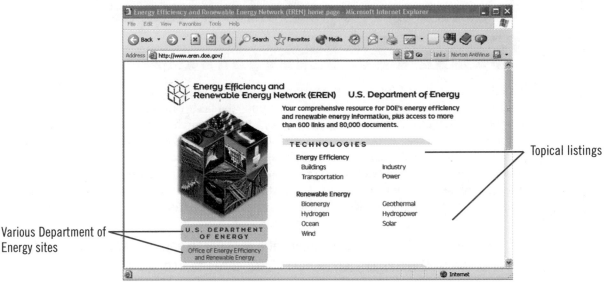

Topical listings

Various Department of Energy sites

FIGURE C-12: EREN's Bioenergy page

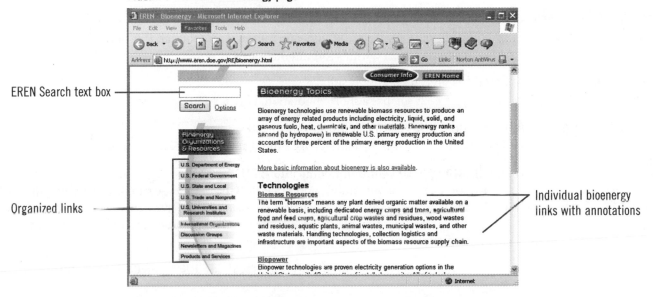

EREN Search text box

Organized links

Individual bioenergy links with annotations

FIGURE C-13: EREN search results

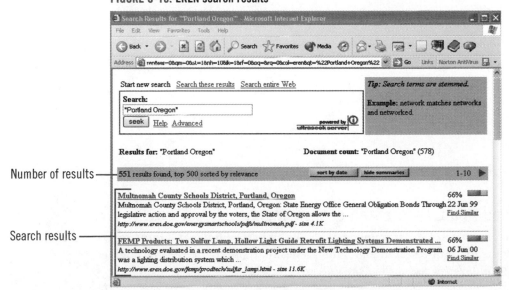

Number of results

Search results

Using Specialized Search Engines

Search engines often find too many results, while subject guides can return too few. There is a compromise that exists on the Web that combines the best features of both: specialized search engines. A **specialized search engine** acts like a normal search engine; for example, you can use Boolean operators to set up a regular search query. However, like subject guides, they limit the Web pages they actually search based on the subject of the search. Specialized search engines are available for a wide variety of topics, from law and medicine, to computers and finance—even energy.  The librarian at the Portland Library has told you that the GEM Database is a good place to locate alternative energy resources on the Web. You decide to see what it offers.

Steps

1. Go to the Student Online Companion at **www.course.com/illustrated/research**, then click the **GEM Database link** (under "Specialized search engines")
   The GEM Database Web page appears, as shown in Figure C-14. You want to find out who sells wind power equipment in the United Sates.

> **QuickTip**
>
> When you submit your search, you may get a Security Information warning. As you are only submitting a search query, click Continue.

2. Scroll down the page and set up a search as shown in Figure C-15 by selecting the appropriate options from the pull-down menus, then click the **Search button**
   A list of results appears, with short annotations.

3. Scroll through the list of results
   Notice that each site has a short annotation, plus a "More Info" link.

> **Trouble?**
>
> If you can't find the California Solar site, try clicking the words "More Info" after another of the listed sites.

4. Click **More Info** for the California Solar site
   The California Solar information page should appear, as in Figure C-16.

5. Scroll through the California Solar information page
   Notice some of the helpful information that the GEM Database supplies, including the URL of the site, a full annotation, the date last checked, the different technologies available, the types of information available at the site, the location of the site, as well as address, phone, and fax information.

6. Answer the question about Appropriateness in the Project File, then save the Project File
   A Web site is appropriate if it answers your initial question.

CLUES TO USE

How do you find a specialized search engine?

Try asking a librarian or professor to recommend a specialized search engine for your research topic. You can also find lists of trailblazer pages, such as the ones listed in the Student Online Companion under the heading "Specialized search engines."

FIGURE C-14: GEM Database Web page

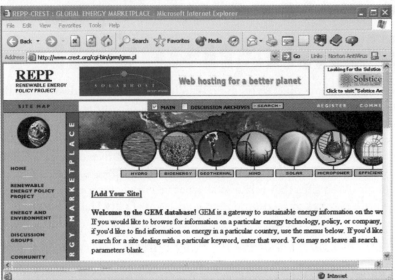

FIGURE C-15: GEM Database search

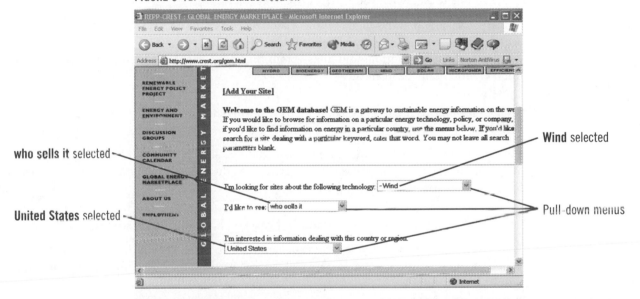

who sells it selected

United States selected

Wind selected

Pull-down menus

FIGURE C-16: California Solar information

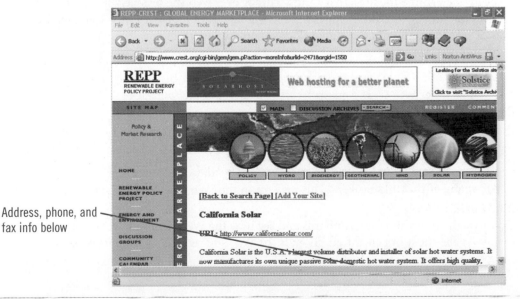

Address, phone, and fax info below

Understanding Evaluative Criteria

No matter what subject you are researching, you should always take the time to evaluate all of the sources of information you find as a result of your search. If anything, you need to be even more critical of information found on the Web than of information found in books. Web information can go directly from the author to you, with no intervening editorial or review process of the kind used for most printed material. **Evaluative criteria** are standards that you can use to determine if a Web site is right for your needs. ◄■■■ You have been running across a lot of different Web sites that relate to alternative energy topics. You need help in determining which are the best ones to recommend to your team at City Hall.

Details

Note: For examples of the following criteria, see Figures C-17 and C-18.

QuickTip

Do the graphics support and enhance the content, or do they just get in the way?

► Organization

The way a Web site is organized is often almost as important as its contents. The following are some questions to ask when you review a Web site:

- Is there a variety of ways to access the material? For example, does the site include a local search engine, topical lists, alphabetical lists, and a site map?
- Do the navigational buttons and links within the Web site get you where you want to go, or are there too many dead ends?

QuickTip

If there is an e-mail link on the page, feel free to write and ask the author questions.

► Authority

Knowing the author's name and qualifications is key to determining how credible or reliable the material is. The following are some questions to ask:

- Can you easily find the author's name, qualifications, and an e-mail link?
- What else has this author written? You may have to do a Web search on his or her name, or look in a book or magazine database.

► Scope

The **scope** of a Web site is the range of topics it covers. The following are some questions to ask:

- Is there an introduction or link to an explanation of the Web site on the home page?
- Where is the Web site hosted? Is it an educational institution, a government site, or a .com (commercial site)?

QuickTip

Is there a bibliography or page that shows the source of the information?

► Objectivity and Accuracy

You can't determine the objectivity and accuracy of a Web site by solely relying on information at the Web site itself. Usually you'll need to validate the information by looking at other Web sites or printed materials. Consider asking the following questions:

- Who is the sponsor of the site? Can you even find the name of the publisher or is it hidden?
- Does the author state the purpose of the site, and his or her bias, openly?
- What do other Web sites or magazine articles say about the sponsor or author?

QuickTip

If the Web page you're looking at is not the site's home page, you may have to look there.

► Currency

If you are looking for historical sources, currency may not be an issue. However, if you are looking for stock quotes or up-to-date computer information, the publication date will matter.

- Look for a "last updated," "created," or "copyright" date.
- Are many of the links broken? This may mean the Web page hasn't been updated lately.

► Appropriateness

Go through all of the above standards and see how the Web site rates. Then you should be able to answer the most important question: Is the Web site right for your purposes?

FIGURE C-17: Solar technology

Sponsoring organization clear

Logical navigation buttons

Copyright date

Author with e-mail link

Appropriate graphic

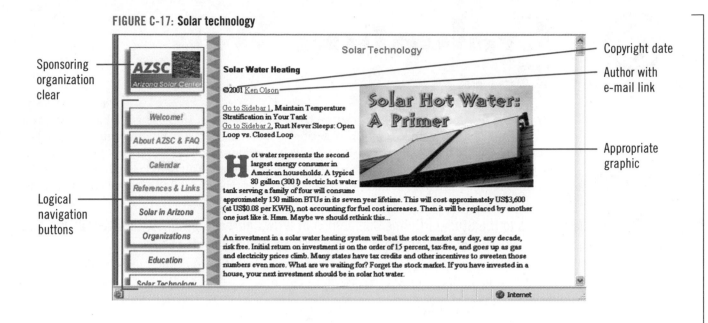

FIGURE C-18: Solar water heating in the United States

Sponsoring organization and mission clear

Authors clearly stated with credentials

Affiliations stated

Well-organized navigation links

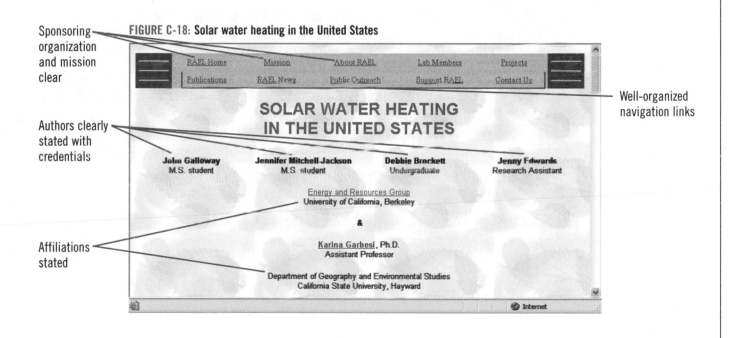

Are there any objective Web sites?

No Web page is totally objective. Remember that commercial sites (.com) always exist to sell something, and non-profit organizations (.org) usually have strong opinions about their causes. The most you can hope for is that these sites divulge their prejudices openly, but you may very often have to "dig around" to find out. Educational (.edu) and government (.gov) sites in general try to be more objective, or at least support their ideas with facts and footnotes. As long as you can ascertain an author's bias, you can come to your own conclusions about the "facts" presented there.

Evaluating Web Pages

Every time you search the Web with a search engine or find Web sites using a subject guide, you will inevitably have to choose which Web sites to investigate. The evaluative criteria in the last lesson are the tools that will enable you to quickly eliminate the least useful sites so that you can focus your time and energy at the most relevant ones. ▬▬▬ You have located a site about the geothermal data. You think it may be relevant to your search but need to evaluate it more closely.

Steps

Trouble?

Has the Geothermal Data site moved or disappeared from the Web? The Student Online Companion will link to a new site and provide new directions to follow.

1. Go to the Student Online Companion at **www.course.com/illustrated/research**, then click the **Geothermal Data link** (under "Specialized search engines")
   The Web page titled "Virginia Tech Geothermal Data WWW Home Page" should appear, as shown in Figure C-19.

2. Scroll through the Web page
   Upon review, you find that the level of writing and its scope are of interest to you. The titles of the topics indicate that it links to some very practical information. You notice the link to Virginia Polytechnic Institute & State University in the first paragraph and decide to follow it in order to learn more about the sponsor of this site.

3. Click the words **Virginia and Polytechnic Institute & State University**
   The Virginia Tech home page should appear, as in Figure C-20. You have verified that the sponsor of the site is a university in Virginia, and you are satisfied that it is a reputable organization. Now you are interested in the author.

4. Click the **Back button** to return to the original Web page, then click the author's name **John K. Costain** near the top of the Web page
   The author's home page should appear, as in Figure C-21. Scrolling through the Web page you notice some impressive accomplishments. You decide to read a bit more about the author.

5. Click the word **Vita** beneath the picture, then scroll through the resulting page
   The author's credentials impress you. You want to see how up-to-date the Web page is.

6. Click the **Back button** 2 times to return to the original Web page, then scroll through the page to see when the page was last updated
   You notice a date at the bottom of the page that is recent enough for your needs.

7. Answer the questions in the Project File, then save and close the Project File

FIGURE C-19: Virginia Tech Geothermal Data home page

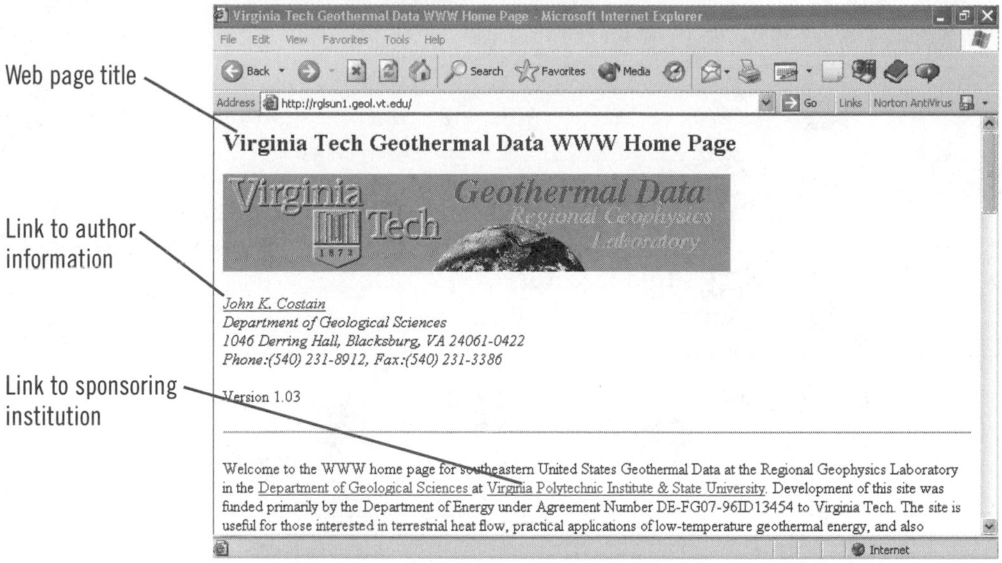

Web page title

Link to author information

Link to sponsoring institution

FIGURE C-20: Virginia Polytechnic and State University home page

Sponsor's name

FIGURE C-21: John K. Costain home page

Practice

► Concepts Review

Label each of the parts of the following subject guide.

FIGURE C-22

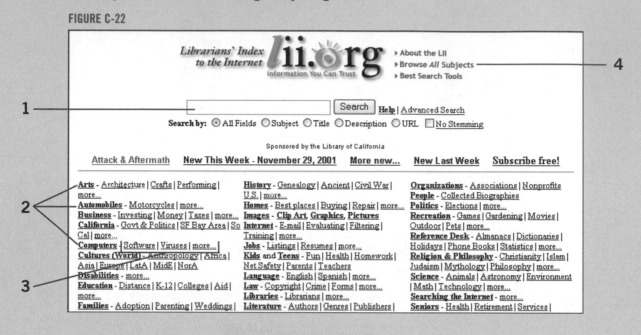

Match each of the following terms with the statement that best describes it.

5. **Hierarchy**

6. **Trailblazer page**

7. **Annotation**

8. **Featured sponsor**

9. **Dewey Decimal**

10. **Site map**

11. **Specialized search engine**

12. **Evaluative criteria**

13. **Distributed**

a. A carefully written summary or review.

b. An advertiser that pays for placement in a subject guide.

c. Standards that help you determine if a Web site is right for you.

d. Often chosen to be included in a subject guide.

e. A term for a subject guide that is compiled by a variety of independent editors.

f. Combines some of the best features of both a subject guide and a search engine.

g. A stratified or ranked order.

h. Classification system used by many libraries and some subject guides.

i. An index to a Web site.

Select the best answer from the list of choices.

14. Subject guides are NOT known as:
a. Subject directories.
b. Search engines.
c. Internet directories.
d. Subject trees.

15. Traits that all subject guides share are:
a. They are organized hierarchically and are selective in the Web sites they list.
b. They are relatively small compared to search engines.
c. They include annotations to the Web sites.
d. All of the above

16. One definition of "browsing" is:
a. Clicking through the hierarchy of topics at a subject guide.
b. Using a local search engine to search a subject guide.
c. Using criteria to evaluate a Web site.
d. Finding out who wrote a Web page.

17. A distributed subject guide:
a. Is maintained by one editor.
b. Usually resides on only one computer.
c. Is the same thing as a search engine.
d. May lack standardization.

18. An annotated subject guide:
a. Allows you to write reviews of Web sites.
b. Contains reviews of Web sites.
c. Reviews other subject guides.
d. Allows you to search for reviews of search engines.

19. A local search engine:
a. Is best searched with complex Boolean queries.
b. Does not usually exist at a subject guide.
c. Will search only in one city or state.
d. Is best searched using one keyword or short phrase.

20. Which is NOT a way subject guides are organized?
a. Alphabetically
b. By hexadecimal
c. By Dewey Decimal
d. Topically

21. Specialized search engines:
   a. Only exist on a few topics.
   b. Are like a regular search engine except they index far more Web pages.
   c. Cannot be queried using Boolean operators.
   d. Share qualities of both subject guides and search engines.

22. Which is a common way to find a specialized Search engine?
   a. Ask a librarian or professor.
   b. See if there is a link to one from a trailblazer page.
   c. Visit a collection of specialized search engines on the Web.
   d. All of the above

23. When evaluating a Web page to determine its authority you do NOT:
   a. Consider the qualifications of the author of a Web page.
   b. Consider the conviction with which an author writes.
   c. Look to see what else the author has written.
   d. Look for biographical information on the author.

Skills Review

1. Understand subject guides.
   a. Open the file called SR-C.rtf from the drive and folder where your Project Files are stored in your text editor or word processor and save it as **Subject Guides SR1.rtf**.
   b. Subject guides share common traits. Choose at least 3 of the 6 common traits mentioned in Lesson One.
   c. Use the Project File to write a few paragraphs about how these traits make subject guides useful for Web research. Mention how they make subject guides different from search engines.
   d. Save the Project File.

2. Browse a subject guide.
   a. You are a woman who has been out of the job market for a few years, and are considering returning to work. You are looking for some information to help you decide what to do.
   b. Open your browser and go to the Student Online Companion at www.course.com/illustrated/research.
   c. Click the About.com link under "Subject guides."
   d. Scan the topical list and follow the Jobs & Careers link. (If an additional window opens when you open About.com, close the window and proceed.)
   e. Follow the link about Career Planning.
   f. Scroll down the Career Planning page and find a link on the left side of the page written specifically for women.
   g. Choose a link from the list of relevant Web sites, then click the title.
   h. Use the Project File to record the title and the URL of the Web site, then save the Project File.

3. Search a subject guide.
   a. You are writing a book and want to avoid plagiarizing the information you read.
   b. Go to the Student Online Companion and click the INFOMINE link.
   c. In the Search text box type **plagiarism**. (*Note:* You may be prompted with a message about submitting insecure information. Close the message window and proceed.)

   d. Use the Project File to record how many relevant Web sites are listed.

   e. Follow a link that you think would be a good one to use.

   f. Use the Project File to record the title and URL, then save the Project File.

4. Navigate a subject guide.

   a. Your little brother is writing a report for his high school Social Studies class about families in the United Kingdom. He has a statistical book that has the Dewey number 310 on it. He asks if you can find more Web information on the same subject.

   b. Open the Student Online Companion and click BUBL LINK /5:15 link.

   c. At the top of the page click **Dewey**.

   d. On the next page click **300 Social sciences**.

   e. On the next page click on **310 Collection of general statistics**.

   f. On the next page click **310 Statistics of the United Kingdom**.

   g. Use the Project File to record the total number of Web sites listed under this Dewey Decimal link.

   h. Browse through the Web sites and their annotations listed at the right of the page. Choose two that you think might be useful for your brother. Use the Project File to record their names and URLs, then save the Project File.

5. Tap a trailblazer page.

   a. You are exploring career choices and have run across The Occupational Outlook Handbook on the Web. You want to decide quickly if this is one that you want to keep in your Favorites (Bookmark) file.

   b. Open the Student Online Companion and click the Occupational Outlook Handbook link under "Specialized search engines." (*Note:* You may be prompted with a message about submitting insecure information. Just close the message and proceed.)

   c. Answer the questions posed in the Project File, then save the Project File.

6. Use a specialized subject search.

   a. Your e-business is thinking of setting up a Web page in France. You'd like to find some facts about how the French use the Internet.

   b. In order to find a specialized search engine, open the Student Online Companion and click the Fossick WebSearch Alliance link (under "Specialized search engines").

   c. Follow the Internet link under the General topic "Computing."

   d. Looking at the specialized search engines available, click **InternetStats.com**. (*Hint:* the InternetStats link may be a little hard to find – it is one of the thumbnail images under "Internet Related Information" near the top of the page.)

   e. On the home page, on the left under "Business Channels," click **INTERNET STATS**.

   f. On the next page click **User Demographics**.

   g. From the list of sites choose **Cyber Atlas**.

   h. In the Search CyberAtlas text box type **France**, then click the Search button.

   i. Answer the questions in the Project File, then save the Project File.

7. Understand evaluative criteria.

   a. Knowing the standards with which to evaluate a Web page is important in helping you efficiently find Web information.

   b. Choose 3 of the 6 evaluation criteria and use the Project File to write a few paragraphs about why they are important. Also include some questions you must ask yourself in relation to these 3 criteria that help you to uncover how relevant the site is to your topic.

   c. Save the Project File.

Internet Research

8. Evaluate a Web page.

    a. You are writing a paper on the history of mathematics. You found a Web page that might be relevant and want to evaluate it quickly.

    b. Open the Student Online Companion, and click the MacTutor History of Mathematics link (under "Specialized search engines").

    c. Answer the questions in the Project File, then save and close the Project File.

▶ Independent Challenge 1

Your company is thinking of expanding its global market. You have been asked to prepare a report on the possibilities of doing business in one of the following countries—Kyrgyzstan, Kuwait, or Jordan. Since the information needs to be reliable, you decide to use the INFOMINE subject guide.

    a. Open the Student Online Companion and click INFOMINE.

    b. Locate the section on **Government Information**.

    c. Find the **Subject List** for Government Information.

    d. From the subject list locate the Web sites about **Kyrgyzstan**, or explore the topic **"Business –Countries"** for links to Kuwait or Jordan.

    e. Find one source that is specific to the topic of business in the country you have chosen.

    f. In a text editor or word processor, write down the name of that Web site and its URL, and write a few sentences about the types of information available at this site.

    g. Add your name to the document, save the file as **Unit C IC1.rtf**, then print it.

▶ Independent Challenge 2

You are beginning a new job working with a team of Web developers. You'd like to find some highly recommended sites that you can bookmark for future use. You are interested in sites about creating Web pages using the Web coding language HTML.

    a. In a text editor of word processor open a new file and save it as **Unit C IC2.rtf**, then go to the Librarians Index to the Internet.

    b. Find their recommended Web sites for HTML.

    c. In the file you created, record how many Web sites they have listed under their topic **"HTML–Document markup language"**. (*Hint:* the number listed under the topic "HTML–Document markup language" is fewer than the number of sites that have HTML in the title or annotation.)

    d. How did you find these sites? In your file, list the steps you took to find them.

    e. Answer the following questions: How many are in the "Best of" category? How many are in the "Specific Resources" category?

    f. Add your name to the document, then save and print the file.

▶ Independent Challenge 3

The health care provider you work for has just made a new Web page. The managers found the Web site shown in Figure C-23 and would like you to evaluate it for them. Is it credible and good enough to include as a link on their Web page? They would like you to have between 5 and 10 reasons why it should be included or not for the next staff meeting.

FIGURE C-23

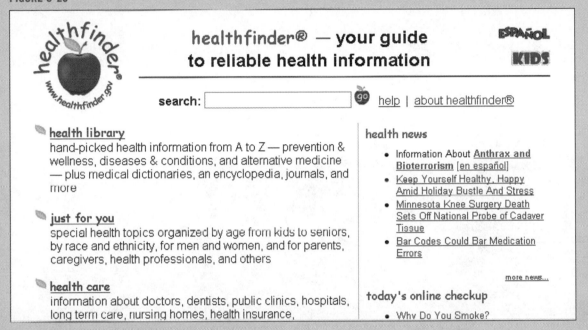

a. Open your browser and find this page on the Web.

b. Evaluate the Web site by asking yourself questions about its organization, authority, scope, objectivity, and currency.

c. In a text editor or word processor, start a new file, save it as **Unit C IC3.rtf**, then write down whether you think this would be an appropriate Web site to link to.

d. Include between 5 and 10 reasons in your argument.

e. Add your name to the document, then save, print, and close it.

▶ Independent Challenge 4

You have an assignment due in one of your classes. You can choose your own subject, but the instructor wants you to use a "credible" Web site as one of your sources. You decide to use a subject guide of academic quality to locate it.

a. Go to one of the following subject guides—Librarian's Index, BUBL, or INFOMINE.

b. Find some sources that you think might be good ones.

c. In a text editor or word processor, start a new file, save it as **Unit C IC4.rtf**, then write down which subject guide you used and how you accessed the sites. (Did you use the local search engine, an alphabetical list, a topical list, etc.?)

d. About how many sites did you find related to your topic?

e. Find one site that you think might be particularly relevant.

f. Evaluate the site according to these criteria: organization, authority, scope, objectivity, and currency.

g. Write a sentence or two explaining how this site rates relative to each of these 5 criteria.

h. Would you say this is an appropriate and credible Web site for your assignment?

i. Add your name to the document, then save, print, and close it.

► Visual Workshop

You are involved in a team who is searching for Web information about alternative energy. A colleague anonymously left the following printout (Figure C-24) from an Internet subject guide called WebBrain on your desk. It looks like a good collection of links to alternative energy sources and you want to locate it. Locate the WebBrain subject guide. Find the page that looks like this one (the number of links you find may be slightly different than the 47 shown, but the configuration on the top will have the same words as the figure). Print a copy of the page and write your name on it.

FIGURE C-24

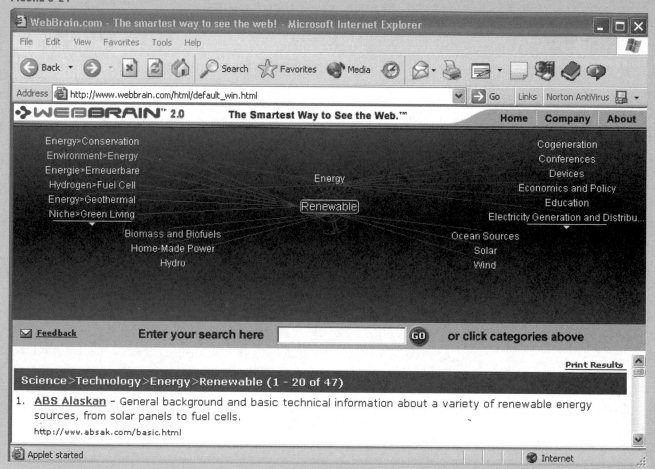

Finding
Specialty Information

Objectives

► **Understand specialized Internet research tools**
► **Find people and places**
► **Locate businesses**
► **Search periodical databases**
► **Find government information**
► **Find online reference sources**
► **Find mailing lists and newsgroups**
► **Search with intelligent agents**

You have already learned to use search engines and subject guides for general research. However, sometimes the information you want is very specific, like someone's name, the address of a business, or the definition of a word. This kind of information is often stored in online databases that require direct access, making traditional search engines and most subject guides ineffective. However, the Web includes **specialized research tools** that give you access to this otherwise inaccessible information. Specialized research tools include online telephone directories, online maps, and online periodicals. There is also a new breed of research tool called an **intelligent agent** that will search for and automatically retrieve information stored in Web databases. Mailing lists and newsgroups can also contain valuable content that you can't access anywhere else on the Web. Knowing how to use these specialized research tools lets you focus your investigation even more. You have been unable to find all of the information you need about alternative energy using search engines and subject guides. You turn your attention to specialized research tools.

Understanding Specialized Internet Research Tools

The search engines that you have used so far have found information only on the **visible Web**, that is, the portion of the Web that is indexed by search engine spiders. However, most Internet content now resides in online databases, unavailable to traditional search engines and subject guides. This "hidden" content is often called the **invisible Web**, or **deep Web**, because it requires a direct query at the database site. Common examples of online databases are online phone books or newspaper and magazine archives. Other examples of inaccessible Web pages are **dynamically generated Web pages** that a database creates based on a specific database query, or pages that require a login name and password. Pages that are not formatted in HTML, like PDF or DOC files, can also be hard for spiders to index. Figure D-1 provides a conceptual diagram of the differences between the invisible and the visible Web. ◄──── Not wanting to ignore a large part of the information available via the Internet, you decide to learn about research tools that will help make the invisible Web visible.

Details

► **Where to find research tools**

Libraries pay for their patrons to use specialized databases, so they are often the first place to look when you want to find a specialty research tool like the full-text magazine and newspaper databases ProQuest, EBSCOhost, and Infotrac. You can also go to a "virtual library" like the Internet Public Library (www.ipl.org), which links to these specialty tools from its reference section.

QuickTip

In order to save time, it's important to read the "About" information at the specialty site before you use it.

► **Scope and focus**

By definition, each specialty tool focuses on one area of the Web. However, even two tools that focus on the same area will not be exactly alike. For example, various governmental agencies are charged with creating access to different, but sometimes overlapping, government information. The National Technical Information Service (NTIS) has a database of publications on scientific, technical, and business-related topics. The U.S. Census Bureau primarily focuses on Web sites containing demographic information, but also features data related to business, as well as Census Bureau products, like CD-ROMs and DVDs for sale. Finally, the Government Printing Office (GPO) is charged with making much of the information produced by the federal government accessible to citizens.

QuickTip

After registering with a "free" site, you may notice an increase in your e-mail. This is the true price you pay for giving the site personal information. This kind of site may start sending you e-mail promotions or may sell your e-mail address to other businesses.

► **Free or pay?**

Many specialty sites are either free or partially free. If they are commercial sites, they may give away some information but charge you for more detailed data. Other sites might allow you free access, but require you to register with them. If a site is going to charge you up-front, it will ask you for your charge card number—so don't give it out unless you want them to use it.

► **Incomplete coverage**

Up-to-date, detailed information about people or businesses is hard to come by and valuable. Many people guard their privacy by choosing not to be included in databases whenever possible, and companies guard proprietary information. For many of your searches, currency will not be an issue. For example, if you are looking for historical information like a quote by Benjamin Franklin, an older version of a book of quotations will suffice. If you suspect your information might not be up to date, make sure to use additional references, including print references, to verify your sources.

► **Automatic searches**

A new breed of research tool called an **intelligent search agent** now makes it possible to automatically retrieve information stored in databases on the Web. An intelligent search agent can simultaneously query hundreds of databases (the invisible Web) as well as traditional online resources (the visible Web). An intelligent search agent "knows" how to query each online database, thus eliminating the need to visit individual sites and manually enter queries. (You still need to manually search specialty databases that require fees or passwords.)

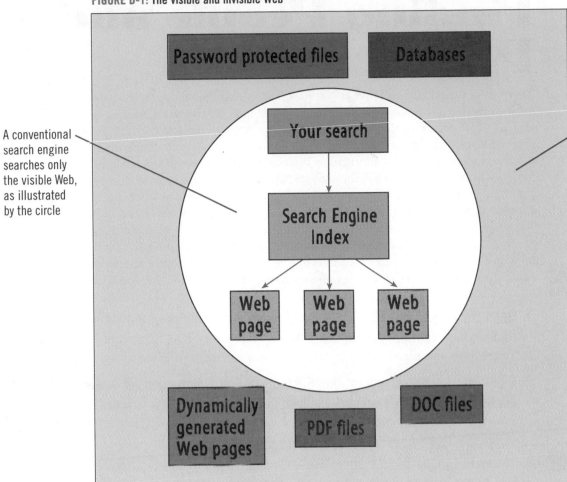

A conventional search engine searches only the visible Web, as illustrated by the circle

The invisible Web is represented by the large box. It is many times larger than the visible Web.

Password protected files

Databases

Your search

Search Engine Index

Web page

Web page

Web page

Dynamically generated Web pages

PDF files

DOC files

CLUES TO USE

Visible and invisible Web

According to a white paper from Bright Planet (makers of LexiBot, an intelligent search agent), the invisible or deep Web is 500 times larger than the visible or surface Web (to see this white paper, click "White Paper: The Deep Web" in the Student Online Companion). The surface Web accounts for only about 1 billion pages, while the deep Web contains approximately 550 billion pages in about 350,000 specialty databases hidden from the view of traditional search engines. Approximately 95 percent of the invisible Web is available publicly (i.e., it doesn't require a fee or password). For more information about the invisible Web, click the links under Invisible Web in the Student Online Companion.

Internet Research

Finding People and Places

There are a variety of "white pages" services on the Web that allow you to search for people. At most of them you can search for a person's phone number and street address. Some white pages sites also allow you to search for e-mail addresses. However, this kind of service is generally more successful at locating phone numbers and street addresses than at finding e-mail addresses. Phone number and street address information is usually based on the information found in telephone books, which tend to be both thorough and accurate. Also, people tend to move less often than they change their e-mail addresses, and there is no real centralized service that gathers e-mail information. The Department of Energy Efficiency and Renewable Energy Network (EREN) is sponsoring a conference in Washington, D.C., for government officials interested in renewable energy. You plan to attend the conference. While you're on the East coast, you also hope to catch up with a relative who you think still lives in New York City. This relative just happens to share your name. You want to find the relative's phone number, street address, and e-mail address.

Steps

1. Open the Project File **IR-D1.rtf** in your word processing program (from the drive and folder where your Project Files are stored), then save it as **Specialty Information.rtf**
   You will use this file to record the information you find in your searches.

2. Open your browser, go to the Student Online Companion at **www.course.com/ illustrated/research**, then click the **Yahoo! People Search link** (under "White Pages")
   The Yahoo! People Search home page appears. You will enter your information in the Telephone Search text boxes, as shown in Figure D-2.

Trouble?

If no names appear, go back to the Search page and try a different name, or leave the First Name field blank.

3. In the Telephone Search area, type your **first name** in the First Name text box; your **last name** in the Last Name text box; **New York** in the City text box; **NY** in the State text box; then click the **Search button**
   A list of names should appear, as shown in Figure D-3. Notice that on the right side of the page, there are links for a "US Search." This kind of search requires you to pay a sum, which is often substantial, by using your credit card online.

4. Choose one name and phone number, then record it in the Project File

5. Click the **name** (it should be underlined on your screen)
   A separate page appears with your person's personal data. Note the links on the left-hand side of the page, which allow you to find businesses in his or her neighborhood, and even a map of the area. You decide to see if you can find an e-mail address.

6. Go to the **Student Online Companion**, then click the **WhoWhere** link (under "White Pages")
   The WhoWhere Web page appears. WhoWhere's database is also created by individuals adding their own information.

Trouble?

Make sure the Search Type says Email.

7. Type your **first name** in the First Name text box, type your **last name** in the Last Name text box, then click the **Search button**
   A list of names may appear, as shown in Figure D-4. If you don't find any results, go back and try the name of the author Robert Schroeder.

QuickTip

There are other e-mail look-up services listed in the Student Online Companion.

8. Scroll through the list, click the words **More Details About** for one of the names, use the Project File to enter the name and e-mail address of the person, then save the Project File
   The name you select may have a little or a lot of information, depending on how much information the person provided. Notice that many of the individual profiles are relatively old.

FIGURE D-2: Yahoo! People Search

Telephone Search area ——

Telephone Search data entry boxes ——

E-mail Search area ——

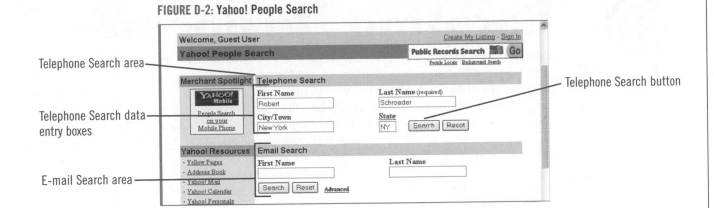

Telephone Search button

FIGURE D-3: Yahoo! People Search results

Details linked to individual names ——

Click "Create My Listing" to add your e-mail information to the database

Links to paid U.S. Search

FIGURE D-4: WhoWhere Search results

More Details link ——

Link to paid U.S. Search ——

Link to High School classmates (free with registration) ——

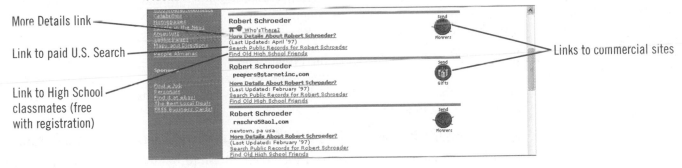

Links to commercial sites

CLUES TO USE

Finding places

Before the advent of the World Wide Web, you had to buy a map or go to the library to find out how to get where you wanted to go. However, the Web now offers quite a few good map and locator Web sites. Many of these sites also provide trip planners and driving directions. In addition, they provide links to hotels, historical sites, and other attractions along the way. The Student Online Companion includes map sites that have driving directions for the United States, such as Maps On Us and Yahoo! Maps. Yahoo! Maps also covers Canada, Spain, Italy, Germany, the UK, and France. MapQuest has sites specific to many countries as well, including the UK (www.mapquest.co.uk), Germany (www.mapquest.de), and France (www.mapquest.fr).

Locating Businesses

Just as there are many sites for finding people and places on the Web, there are also many "yellow pages" sites for finding businesses in the United States and worldwide, as shown in Table D-1. The site AnyWho (listed in the Student Online Companion) provides a list of international directories. The most high-powered business finders, like Switchboard, integrate business directory listings with maps and travel planners. Most of the yellow pages directories on the Web build their databases from accurate and up-to-date information and allow new businesses to add their own information at any time. There is no charge to a business for the basic address and telephone listings. However, if a business wants to include a link to its Web site or an advertisement, it is charged for the service. ✒ While you are at the conference in Washington, D.C., you plan to meet with a solar energy researcher. You want to find out where her office is located. You remember that the name of the company is something like "Observation Energy," and you think it's in Arlington, Virginia.

Steps

1. Go to the Student Online Companion at **www.course.com/illustrated/research**, then click the **Switchboard link** (under "Yellow Pages")
   The Switchboard Web site appears. You can use this Web site to find a person, a business, or a product.

2. On the left side of the page, click the words **Find a Business**
   The Switchboard business search page appears.

3. In the Type of Business text box, type **solar**, in the City text box type **Arlington**, in the State text box type **VA** (as shown in Figure D-5), then click the **Search button**
   A list of different types of solar-related businesses appears. Since the business you are looking for is a research company, you decide to choose Solar Energy Research & Development.

4. Click **Solar Energy Research & Development**
   A list of businesses appears, as shown in Figure D-6. The Switchboard search didn't take your entire search input literally; it searched for businesses *near* Arlington, Virginia, rather than restricted to Arlington, Virginia, and found Observatory Solar Energy Co. on Wisconsin Ave. in Washington, D.C. This is the business you are looking for.

5. Record the business address in the Project File
   Since you'll be in the area around lunchtime, you want to see what restaurants are nearby. You notice that the link includes options called Map, Directions, and What's Nearby. Switchboard is a thorough site.

6. Click the **What's Nearby** link below the Observatory Solar Energy information, scroll down the page shown in Figure D-7, then click the word **Restaurants** under Eateries
   Ignore the advertisements on the right-hand side of the page. These restaurants aren't necessarily nearby; they've just paid to be put on the Web page.

7. Choose a restaurant from the list that appears on the left side of the page, record the name and address in the Project File, then save the Project File

QuickTip

Notice that some of your initial assumptions, that this business was in *Arlington* and named *Observation*, were wrong. However, you still found what you were looking for because Switchboard took your information and searched for any data that *approximately* matched what you were looking for. In a database like Switchboard, *not* entering all your data at once can sometimes be a good search strategy!

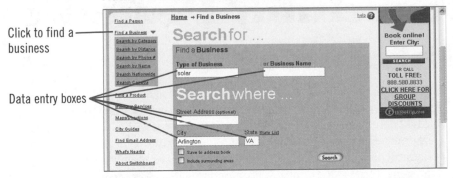

Click to find a business

Data entry boxes

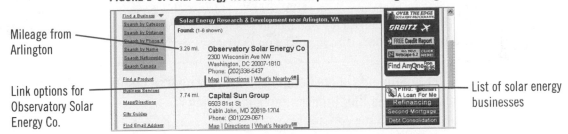

Mileage from Arlington

Link options for Observatory Solar Energy Co.

List of solar energy businesses

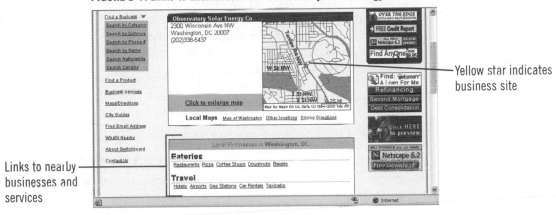

Yellow star indicates business site

Links to nearby businesses and services

TABLE D-1: Features of business finder Web sites (see Student Online Companion)

name/url	countries covered	people	businesses	products	toll-free numbers	maps	city pages
AnyWho	USA	X	X		X		
Canada411	Canada	X	X				
Europages	30 European Countries		X	X			
Scoot	Belgium, the Netherlands, France,& the UK	X					
SuperPages	USA	X	X			X	X
Switchboard	USA	X	X	X		X	X
Ukphonebook	UK	X	X				
Yell.com	UK		X				
Yellowpages.ca	Canada	X	X		X		X
Yellowpages.com.au	Australia	X	X			X	

Searching Periodical Databases

Some of the most authoritative and current information hidden in the invisible Web is stored in periodical databases. These include the archives of popular magazines, newspapers, and scholarly journals. Table D-2 describes the differences between different types of periodicals and gives examples of each type. Some periodicals, like *Salon* or *First Monday*, exist only in electronic format on the Web. Other periodicals, like *The Times* or *The New York Times*, have an online version that may or may not carry all the same stories as the printed version, and may include some stories not seen in print. There are also subscription databases like ProQuest and InfoTrac, available at libraries, which store electronic versions of thousands of periodical titles. Most online periodical databases will give out limited recent information for free, but require registration or payment for older materials. You decide to look for some current articles on alternative energy topics.

1. Go to the Student Online Companion at **www.course.com/illustrated/research**, then click **The Times link** (under "Periodical listings")

The Times Web site appears.

2. Type **energy** in the **Search this site text box**, then click the **Go button**

A new browser window with links to relevant articles should appear, as in Figure D-8. Near the bottom of the page, note the message under "SEARCH TIPS" stating that articles published within the last seven days are free, but there is a charge for older articles. A percentage figure appears beside each article indicating the article's relevance to your search. You want to read an article.

3. Click the **title** of an article, scan the article, **close** the two top windows, then answer the questions in the Project File

Next, you want to try searching a larger periodical database.

4. Go to the **Student Online Companion**, then click the **MagPortal.com link**

The MagPortal site appears. Notice the broad topical categories and the pull-down menu that lets you sort your results in a variety of ways.

5. Type **"renewable energy"** in the Search text box, then click the **Search button**

A list of online articles appears, as shown in Figure D-9. Notice some features of this search results page. The "Related Categories" are links to topics that contain related articles. Down the left side are links to the online publications and the dates of the articles. The article title and an annotation appear in the center of the page. The wavy line at the end of each article links you to similar articles.

6. Click the **title** of one of the articles

You should be taken from the MagPortal Web site to the publication site.

7. Answer the questions in the Project File, then save the Project File

Trouble?

Did your search find any articles? If not, try another search using another alternative energy topic or a topic that you know has been in the international news lately. If your search still does not yield any articles, continue to Step 4 after typing "No articles found" in the Project File. If a login box opens for the article you choose, close it and click the title of a different article.

CLUES TO USE

Where to find online periodicals

There are some sites on the Web that are "online newsstands." They collect links to electronic periodicals from around the world on all topics. Examples are provided in the Student Online Companion. They include the Internet Public Library Online Serials collection, the Librarians' Index to the Internet Magazine Topics, and NewsDirectory.com. Other sites like MagPortal.com and FindArticles create portals where you can search many online magazine databases simultaneously. The most comprehensive online databases like ProQuest and InfoTrac are available through public, school, and academic libraries. As long as you are affiliated with a library you can access these databases from home at no charge — just ask your local librarian how.

Percentage indicates article's relevance to your search

Click title to open article

See SEARCH TIPS near bottom of page

FIGURE D-9: MagPortal article list

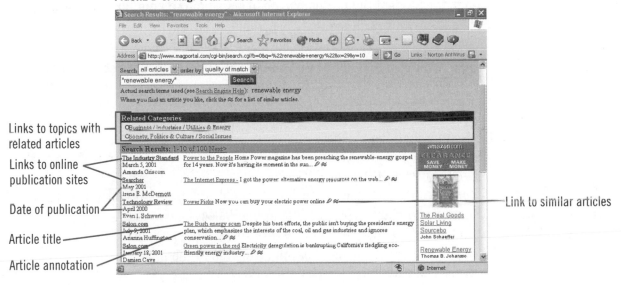

Links to topics with related articles

Links to online publication sites

Date of publication

Article title

Article annotation

Link to similar articles

TABLE D-2: Periodicals and their distinguishing characteristics

type of periodical	purpose	publisher	audience / language	documentation	examples
Scholarly research	Reports original research or experiments	A university or professional organization	Other scholars / scholarly and subject-specific	Citations and bibliography	*Harvard Education Review*
Professional/ specialized interest	Communicate professional practices	A professional organization or commercial publisher	Professionals / technical	May cite, but often personal experience	*Journal of Accountancy*
Substantive general interest	To provide information to a broad audience	A commercial publisher	Educated / somewhat technical	May mention sources, seldom cites	*The New York Times*
Popular	To entertain or promote a viewpoint	A commercial publisher	General audience / simple language	Rarely cites	*Family Circle*

Internet Research

Finding Government Information

Governments are prodigious producers and users of information. Large gateways, called **portals**, create access to different segments of government information, as shown in Table D-3. Portals originated in the commercial sector. They were sites like America Online and MSN that offered "everything" — search engines, news, shopping, e-mail, chat, and more. They each endeavored to create such an attractive and useful site that you would never go anywhere else to find information. The idea of a portal caught on and now many other sites have carved out niches in various subject areas, especially in industry and government. These portals, which are limited by subject, are also referred to as **vortals**, or vertical portals. Government portals can give you access to online information or to printed materials that you can purchase from government agencies or borrow from libraries. While you were at the EREN conference in Washington, D.C., you learned about a good place to access government information online. You want to see if the Web site FirstGov can help you in your research. You also want to see if you can find information about a project you've recently heard about, called "Million solar roofs."

Steps

1. Go to the Student Online Companion at **www.course.com/illustrated/research**, then click the **FirstGov link** (under "Government references")
   The FirstGov Web site appears. You will use the topic of "solar energy" as a test case.

2. Type **"solar energy"** in the Search text box, then click the **Search button**
   A list of search results appears, as shown in Figure D-10. Note that FirstGov searched for federal information because "Federal" was selected by default. Your general search found over 1,000 results.

3. Scroll through the results
   You notice a few nice features, like the "tips" link to help you narrow your search, and the annotations for each of the Web sites.

4. From the list of results, find the **National Renewable Energy Laboratory (NREL) Home Page**, then record the URL in the Project File
   You want to search for the "Million solar roofs" project you heard about.

5. Click the words **Advanced Search** at the top of the page
   The FirstGov Advanced Search form appears.

6. From the first pull-down menu, choose **The Exact Phrase** option, type **million solar roofs** in the Search text box, then click the **Submit button**
   A long list of relevant search results appears. You want to see how well FirstGov works at the state level.

7. Click the **New Search button**
   A blank Advanced Search form appears. You decide to search for information about wind turbines in Oregon.

8. From the first pull-down menu, choose **The Exact Phrase** option, type **wind turbines** in the Search text box, then click the **Add More Terms button**
   The search form expands to include a text box for additional information. The text box appears under the words "In addition." You will add information to your search, as shown in Figure D-11.

9. Type **Oregon** in the new search text box, click **State**, then click the **Submit button**
   A list of results appears.

10. Use the Project File to record the URL of the **Oregon Office of Energy**, then save the Project File

QuickTip

Make sure the Project File is still open in your word processor.

FIGURE D-10: Solar energy search results

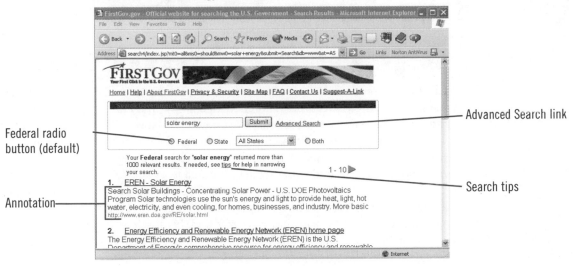

Advanced Search link

Federal radio
button (default)

Search tips

Annotation

FIGURE D-11: Advanced Search for wind turbines in Oregon

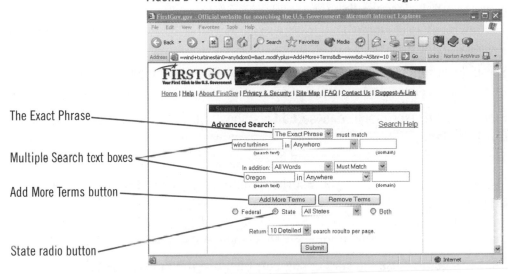

The Exact Phrase

Multiple Search text boxes

Add More Terms button

State radio button

TABLE D-3: Specialized government portals (see Student Online Companion)

name/url	features
Australian Commonwealth Government Information	• Australian federal and state information
Canadian Government Information on the Internet	• Canadian federal, provincial, and municipal information
FedWorld (US)	• Sponsored by the National Technical Information Service (NTIS) Includes scientific, technical, and engineering information Most links are to reports and publications for purchase Some links are to government Web sites
FirstGov (US)	• Most comprehensive site for U.S. government information online Over 20,000 links to government Web sites U.S. federal and state information
Ukonline (UK)	• Central and local government information for the United Kingdom
United States Government Printing Office	• Links to federal publications online, especially to U.S. legal and Congressional information Catalog of U.S. government documents for sale Catalog of libraries across the U.S. that own specific documents
University of Michigan Documents Center	• Most complete guide to government information Local, state, federal, foreign, and multinational government links

Unit D

Internet Research

Finding Online Reference Sources

Online reference sources are similar to their counterparts on library shelves. They include almanacs, dictionaries, directories, and encyclopedias — the kinds of references you don't read cover to cover, but refer to often. Library Web sites almost always link to a variety of online reference sources, some of them licensed exclusively for their patrons' use. There are also virtual libraries, like the Internet Public Library, that exist solely to bring together valuable Web sites and reference tools. It's a good idea, once you've found a few good reference sites, to include them in your browser's Favorites or Bookmarks file for easy access. ➤ You are beginning to summarize the information you've been finding on the Web about alternative energy sources. You still need to find some reliable statistical resources and, because some of the sites you've found are technical in nature, you want to link to a site that converts units to their metric equivalents.

Steps

1. Go to the Student Online Companion at **www.course.com/illustrated/research**, then click the **IPL Reference link** (under "Online references")

The Internet Public Library Online Serials page appears. You want to see if it includes any statistical resources relating to energy.

2. Scroll down the page and click **Census Data & Demographics**

A long list of sources appears. You decide you just want to locate sources relating to energy.

> **Trouble?**
>
> Netscape 4.x users can choose Edit, then choose Find in Page. Netscape 6.x users can choose Search, then choose Find in This Page.

3. From your browser menu, choose **Edit** as shown in Figure D-12, then choose **Find (on This Page)**

The Find dialog box appears, as shown in Figure D-13.

4. In the Find what text box, type **energy**, then click the **Find Next button** (or the **Find button** in Netscape)

Your browser highlights the word *energy* in the annotation to a Web site called Statistical Resources on the Web. After reading the annotation, you decide this looks like a good site.

> **Trouble?**
>
> If the site you found was *not* Statistical Resources on the Web, try clicking the **Find Next** or **Find** button again until you find it. If you don't find it, just locate an appropriate substitute.

5. Click **Cancel** to close the Find dialog box, then use the Project File to record the URL of the **Statistical Resources on the Web** site

Because many of the energy Web pages you've encountered have been located in Europe, you're hoping to find a site that will make conversions from the metric system to the English system.

6. Click the browser **Back button** to return to the IPL Reference Resources page, scroll down the page, then click **Calculation & Conversion Tools**

A list of calculation tools appears at the Internet Public Library site.

7. Scroll down the page, click **A Dictionary of Measures, Units and Conversions**, scroll down the resulting page, then click **by Volume** under Specific Energy

The Specific Energy (by volume) Calculator appears. You want to test it by entering the information shown in Figure D-14.

8. In the Type in size text box, type **50000**, choose **BTU/gallon(US)** from the select units pull-down menu, then click **Convert It!**

50,000 BTUs per gallon is instantly converted into a variety of international units. You decide this is a good site to visit again in the future.

9. Use the Project File to record the number of kilojoules per cubic meter (kJ/cu.metre) on the results page, then save the Project File

FIGURE D-12: Find (on This Page) menu option

Browser Edit option

Find (on This Page) option

FIGURE D-13: The Find dialog box

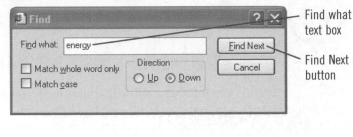

Find what text box

Find Next button

FIGURE D-14: Specific energy by volume Search

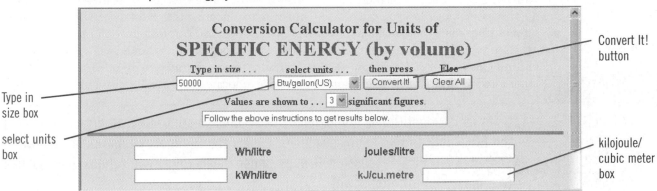

Convert It! button

Type in size box

select units box

kilojoule/ cubic meter box

Online reference sources about the Internet

The Web includes reference sources on just about any topic. If you are working on a special research topic, you can always find good sources at the Reference sections of the Internet Public Library or the Librarians' Index to the Internet and add them temporarily to your browser's Bookmark (Favorite) files. For instance, if you were studying the Internet, the following might be good sources to have close at hand:

name	type of resource	features
FILExt	Dictionary	• Lists most of the file extensions encountered on the Internet • Defines the extensions and often links to more information
Netiquette Home Page	Online book	• The basics of Netiquette, as well as Netiquette at home and at work • Primarily covers e-mail and discussion groups
Webopedia	Dictionary/encyclopedia	• Covers computer and Internet terminology • Short one to two paragraph definitions with links
Living Internet	Encyclopedia	• Covers the Internet, the Web, e-mail, chat, newsgroups, and mailing lists • Thorough articles that include history and how to use the various facets of the Net
Internet Tutorials (at the University at Albany Libraries)	Online tutorials	• Topics include Using and Searching the Web; Browsers; and Software Training
Librarians' Index to the Internet — Internet Topics Page	Subject guide	• Great links that will answer almost any Internet question

Finding Mailing Lists and Newsgroups

The Internet is more than just its Web documents; it also provides a variety of ways to communicate and interact with other people. On the Web, you can instantly become part of discussions of current issues and breaking news by subscribing to a **mailing list**, which allows you to e-mail messages to all other members of the list automatically. Mailing lists are often called **listservs** after the software that supports them. Another major method of information exchange on the Internet is **newsgroups**, virtual bulletin boards where messages on thousands of topics are posted daily. Newsgroups are often referred to as **Usenet** after the system that distributes them. Anyone on the Internet can read and respond to the postings in a newsgroup. As the posted topics diverge, they are broken off into different **threads**, or sub-topics. By searching the archives of discussion postings, you can also tap into primary documents that follow the development of topics from many personal and unconventional angles. You can find links to mailing lists and news groups about specific subjects on trailblazer Web pages, or you can search specific sites that list mailing lists or newsgroups. ✒ You want to communicate with other people who are interested in alternative energy topics. You decide to locate some mailing lists and news groups.

Steps

1. Go to the Student Online Companion at **www.course.com/illustrated/research**, click the **EREN link** (under "Subject guides"), click the **Bioenergy link** under Renewable Energy, then click **Discussion Groups** under Bioenergy Organizations & Resources (you may need to scroll down)
A page of links to newsgroups and mailing lists appears, as shown in Figure D-15.

Trouble?

The subscription address will have the form *listname-subscribe@someplace.org*.

2. Click a **mailing list** that seems interesting, find the **subscription address** at its Web site, then use the Project File to record the address

3. Go to the **Student Online Companion**, click the **Google link** (under "Search engines"), then click the **Groups tab**
Note that there is a Search text box where you can search the archives of Usenet postings with keywords. You decide that your topic, alternative energy, probably is listed under **sci**.

QuickTip

Newsgroup names are hierarchical and mnemonic. For example, a recreational group that discusses the *game* of *chess* might be called *rec.games.chess*. The different parts of the name are separated by periods.

4. Click the word **sci**.
Groups that have the prefix **sci** are the science-related newsgroups. The bars to the left of the names of the newsgroups indicate the relative volume of messages posted.

5. **Scroll** down the page and click the words **sci.energy**
A list of postings to the sci.energy newsgroup appears, as shown in Figure D-16. This is the archive of the various newsgroup threads.

QuickTip

If you wanted to participate in any of the threads at sci.energy, you could click "Post a new message to sci.energy." You would need to register and obtain a password first in order to be able to post.

6. **Scroll** down the page and find a thread of interest to you, then answer the questions in the Project File
You are interested in reading more about the uses and development of Usenet Newsgroups.

7. Go to the **Student Online Companion**, click the **Development of Usenet link** (under "Online references"), read the article entitled "The Social Forces Behind the Development of Usenet," answer the question in the Project File, then save and close the Project File

FIGURE D-15: Bioenergy discussion groups

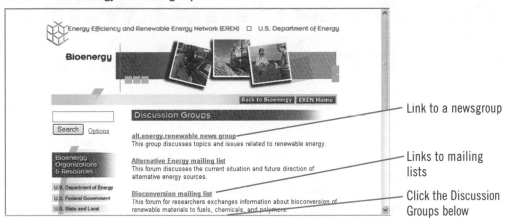

Link to a newsgroup

Links to mailing lists

Click the Discussion Groups below

FIGURE D-16: Postings at the sci.energy newsgroup

Newsgroup name

Number of threads in newsgroup

Posting dates

Thread subjects

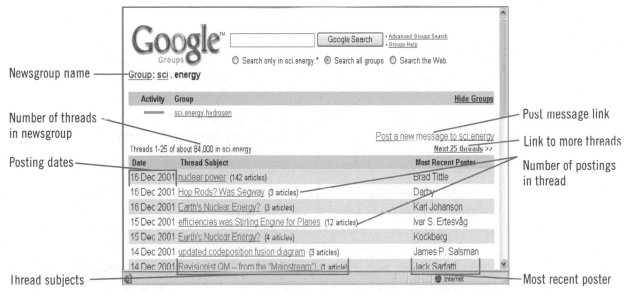

Post message link

Link to more threads

Number of postings in thread

Most recent poster

Netiquette

Netiquette is the word Internet users use to describe the protocol and common rules of courtesy used by people on the Internet. For example, when you use a mailing list, you need to know that there are two separate e-mail addresses that have very different functions. You use the **subscription address** (a.k.a. "administrative address") to send messages asking the administrator to add or drop your name from the list. The **list address** is the place to send your actual list correspondence. If you use the wrong address and send your subscription information to the 10,000 or more members of a list, more than one may e-mail you and politely let

you know that you should use the *other* address. (If any member e-mails you and *impolitely* tells you to use the other address, this is called a "flame.")

You should also know that before you post to a newsgroup, it is good form to read the FAQ (frequently asked questions) and some of the more recent postings. In this way you will insure that you don't post a message to an inappropriate group, or ask a question that has been answered in a recent thread. For more information on netiquette, click the Netiquette Home Page link under "Online references" in the Student Online Companion.

Searching with Intelligent Agents

As the Internet grows and becomes more diverse, finding the correct information is more of a challenge. Fortunately, new tools are evolving that make searching the visible and invisible parts of the Web simpler and more comprehensive. An **intelligent search agent**, or **search bot**, is a software program that automates search activities that traditional search services aren't programmed to perform, such as searching through online databases. One of the most powerful intelligent search agents is **LexiBot**, which can simultaneously query 150 databases, search engines, and subject guides out of a possible 2,200. LexiBot "knows" how to query each database, eliminating the need to visit individual sites and manually enter queries. In addition, LexiBot can sort and analyze search results from multiple sources, making it faster and easier to find the information you need. ➤ You want to explore how an intelligent agent can make your searching more efficient and effective. You decide to see how well LexiBot can locate the latest information about alternative energy.

Steps

Trouble?

If LexiBot isn't installed on your computer, please see the Read This Before You Begin page.

1. **Start LexiBot**
   The LexiBot License Agreement dialog box appears.

2. **Read the license agreement, click Accept, then maximize LexiBot**
   LexiBot appears in full screen mode, as shown in Figure D-17. Table D-3 provides a brief description of LexiBot's main screen controls. Since you are looking for recent information about alternative energy, you decide to have LexiBot query news sources.

3. **Click Search on the Menu bar, then click Select Web Sources to Search**
   The Select Web Sources to Search dialog box opens, with options for adding topics to the sources to be searched. The Topic Groups pane on the left contains a list of additional searchable sources, organized into groups.

QuickTip

You can choose an entire group or individual sources from a group to include in your search. Click the plus sign (+) to the right of a group to expand and display the sources belonging to that group. Click the minus sign (-) to collapse and hide the list.

4. **Scroll down the Topic Groups pane to News, click News, click the right pointing arrow between the Topic Groups and Sources panes, then click Done**
   All the sources in the News topic appear in the Sources pane before the dialog box closes. These news sources will now be searched, along with the default engines.

5. **In the Query Box, type "alternative energy" OR "alternative power", then click the Search button**
   The status bars at the bottom of the main screen indicate the progress of the search as LexiBot attempts to download all the pages found in the search.

6. **When the search finishes, click OK in the Search Completed dialog box**
   The Results Window displays the search results, as shown in Figure D-18. The Score column displays results in descending order, with pages most closely matching your query at the top.

7. **Double-click the top page in your Results Window, then when the Confirm View with Browser dialog box opens, click OK**
   Your browser opens and displays the page. To share your search results with colleagues, you decide to save them as a Web page.

QuickTip

To find out more about intelligent search agents, or search bots, go to the Student Online Companion and click either BotKnowledge or BotSpot: Search bots.

8. **Close your browser, click File on the LexiBot menu bar, point to Export Results, click Displayed Results as a Web Page, type Alternative energy in the File name text box, use the Save in text box to select a drive and/or folder to store the Web page, then click the Save button**

9. **Print the Web page from your browser, write your name at the top of the printout, close the browser, click File on the menu bar of LexiBot, click Exit, then click OK in the File Not Saved dialog box**
   LexiBot closes without saving your search results.

FIGURE D-17: LexiBot

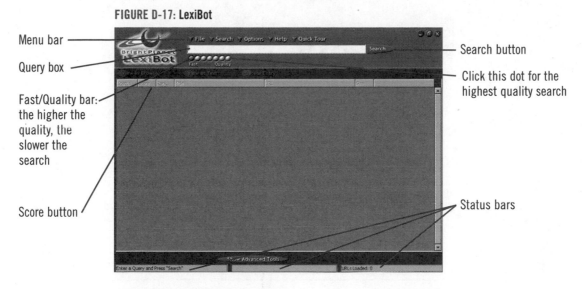

Menu bar

Query box

Fast/Quality bar: the higher the quality, the slower the search

Score button

Search button

Click this dot for the highest quality search

Status bars

FIGURE D-18: LexiBot Search results

TABLE D-3: LexiBot main screen controls

control	description	control	description
Menu bar	*File* - commands to open, save, and export result *Search* - commands for determining where and how to search *Options* - viewing and ranking pages, Internet connections, manual settings, and preference settings *Help* - assistance for using, updating, and registering *Quick Tour* - instructions on how to use LexiBot	**Results Window buttons**	*View in Browser* - displays selected page in your browser *View as Text* - displays selected page in LexiBot browser window—text only *Delete Entry* - removes selected page *Mark* - indicates pages to be used in re-ranking *Re-Rank* - rearranges results with marked pages *Add Note* - allows annotation of pages
Query box	Enter search statement here	**Search button**	Start the query process
Search Target buttons	Select the top button, just to the right of the Query Box to search Web resources. Click the bottom button to the right of the Query Box to query a previous search.	**Fast/Quality bar**	Clicking a position further to the right returns a higher number of results that better match your query. Clicking the right-most position yields the best search results. However, the higher the quality, the slower the search.
Status bar	Shows the progress of the current search	**Show/Hide Advanced Tools button**	Displays/removes Advanced Tools from main screen

Internet Research

Practice

► Concepts Review

Label each of the elements of the Usenet newsgroup archive page.

FIGURE D-19

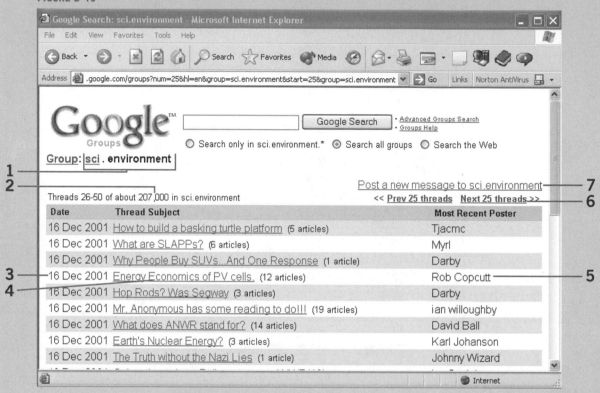

Match each term with the statement that describes it.

8. Visible Web

9. Dynamic Web page

10. White pages

11. Yellow pages

12. Internet Public Library

13. Portal

14. Mailing list

15. Newsgroup

16. Intelligent search agent

a. Web sites with "people finder" tools.

b. An example of a virtual library.

c. A gateway to large segments of related Web information.

d. An Internet bulletin board.

e. A software program that automates search activities.

f. Allows you to send and receive e-mail to and from a group of subscribers.

g. The portion of the Web accessible to Search engine indexing programs.

h. Web sites that help you find businesses.

i. A Web page that is generated when you ask for it.

Select the best answer from the list of choices.

17. The invisible Web:
   a. Is not accessible.
   b. Consists mostly of pages written in HTML.
   c. Is much smaller than the visible Web.
   d. Is also known as the deep Web.

18. You would not usually access specialty research tools by:
   a. Asking a librarian.
   b. Using a search engine.
   c. Using a library's Web site.
   d. Using a virtual library site.

19. Specialty sites may:
   a. Require you to pay for the service.
   b. Allow you a few free searches and ask you to pay for more.
   c. Give away some information but charge for some too.
   d. All of the above

20. One reason that online coverage can be incomplete is:
   a. Companies like to give out proprietary information.
   b. Copyright law allows anyone to put current editions online.
   c. Many people value their privacy.
   d. New information has little value in today's marketplace.

21. You would usually look for _____ at an online White pages site.
   a. A person's address
   b. A person's e-mail address
   c. A person's phone number
   d. All of the above

22. A good place to search for information about businesses in the UK and France is:
   a. The Librarian's Index to the Internet.
   b. Scoot.
   c. Yellowpages.ca.
   d. Switchboard.

23. The sub-topics that appear within a newsgroup are called:
   a. Threads.
   b. Mailing lists.
   c. Listservs.
   d. Usenets.

24. A site that links to local, state, federal, foreign, and multinational government links is:
   a. FirstGov.
   b. University of Michigan Documents Center.
   c. FedWorld.
   d. United States Government Printing Office.

25. LexiBot is an example of:
   a. A search engine.
   b. A subject guide.
   c. An intelligent search agent.
   d. A Yellow pages site.

26. When searching with LexiBot, the relationship between speed and quality is:
   a. The higher the quality, the slower the search.
   b. The higher the quality, the faster the search.
   c. The lower the quality, the slower the search.
   d. None of the above

Skills Review

Reminder: You can access all of the Web sites in the Skills Review from the Student Online Companion at
www.course.com/illustrated/research.

1. Understand other Internet research tools.
   a. Open the Project File SR-D.rtf from the drive and location where your Project Files are stored and save it as **Invisible Web.rtf**.
   b. Use the Project File to write a paragraph or two about the nature of the invisible Web and how specialty research tools work.

2. Find people.
   a. Go to the Yahoo! People Search page.
   b. Type your name (or a friend's name) into the appropriate Telephone Search text boxes.
   c. Click the Search button.
   d. Click your name (or your friend's name) on the results page.
   e. Print the resulting page of information and put your name on the top.

3. Locate a business.
   a. Go to the Switchboard site and click the Find a Business link on the left-hand side of the page.
   b. Type a Type of Business (or a Business Name), a City, and State.
   c. Click an appropriate business category on the resulting page. (If there are no resulting businesses, go back and choose another type of business.)
   d. Scroll down the results page and find a business located in the city you chose.
   e. Click the Map link.
   f. Print the map and add your name to the top. (You may need to click the "Printable Map" link near the bottom of the map to get a good copy.)

4. **Search periodical databases.**
   a. Click the MagPortal link at the Student Online Companion.
   b. Search for a magazine article by typing your search terms in the Search text box.
   c. Scan over the list of resulting articles and answer the question posed in the Project File.
   d. Click the FindArticles link at the Student Online Companion.
   e. Search for another article on the same topic.
   f. Scan the list of resulting articles at FindArticles and follow the instructions in the Project File.
   g. Save and close the Project File.

5. **Find government information.**
   a. Go to the FirstGov site.
   b. Type Senator in the Search text box, choose State, then choose a state name from the pull-down menu.
   c. Click the Search button.
   d. Find a Web page with a state senator's name on it.
   e. Print the Web page and add your name to the top.

6. **Locate online reference services.**
   a. Go to the Internet Public Library Reference Resources page.
   b. Click the Style & Writing Guides link.
   c. Scroll down the page and click the Citing Electronic Resources link.
   d. Find a Web site that will help you cite documents in the APA style.
   e. Click the page name, print a copy, and add your name to the top of the page.

7. **Find a newsgroup.**
   a. Go to the Google Search engine and click the Groups tab.
   b. Click a type of group of interest to you (biz., comp., sci., etc.).
   c. Choose a subgroup and click it (biz.ecommerce, comps.emace, etc.).
   d. Find a thread of interest to you, and click that thread.
   e. Print the resulting archived message and add your name to the top.

8. **Search with an intelligent agent.**
   a. Launch LexiBot.
   b. Type a search in the Search text box and click the "Fast" button, if necessary.
   c. Click the Search button.
   d. Make sure the search results are ranked from highest to lowest (you may have to click the Score button).
   e. Print the first page of your search results and add your name to the top of the page.

▶ Independent Challenge 1

You and a business associate are driving from London to York to visit some clients. As you haven't driven there before, you want to get driving directions.

    a. Go to MapQuest UK.

    b. Find the section for driving directions.

    c. Enter the appropriate to and from locations and get the directions.

    d. On the resulting directions page, locate the "Redisplay Directions with" section and choose Text Only.

    e. Print a copy of the directions, and add your name to the top of the page.

▶ Independent Challenge 2

You are on an airplane flying to Sydney NSW Australia on business. You are with a firm that specializes in designing Web sites for banks. Your company is going to design the Web site for the Waratah Mortgage Corporation, and you decide to look on the Internet to see if there are other banks in Sydney that you might visit while you are there. You want to look up phone numbers and locations of some banks on your laptop.

    a. Go to an appropriate Yellow pages directory.

    b. From the information you know, set up an appropriate search.

    c. Find two banks that are located in Sydney.

    d. Print a map of each of their locations and put your name on top.

▶ Independent Challenge 3

You are thinking of immigrating to Canada and starting a business. You have heard there is a special "business class" immigration available.

    a. Go to an appropriate government Web site.

    b. Locate an official Canadian government Web page that has the information you need.

    c. Print the page and add your name to the top.

▶ Independent Challenge 4

You want to learn more about the content "hidden" in databases on the Internet. Since news articles about the invisible or deep Web are likely to be stored (or hidden) in magazine archives (databases), you decide to use the intelligent search agent LexiBot to search both the invisible (deep) Web, as well as the visible Web.

a. Open LexiBot.

b. To search magazine archives with LexiBot, open the Select Web Sources to Search dialog box, scroll down the Topic Groups pane to Magazines and eZines, add this topic to the Sources pane, and click Done.

c. In the Query Box, type **"invisible Web" OR "deep Web"** and then click the **Search** button. (*Note:* Depending on the speed of your modem and/or the speed of your connection, LexiBot can take up to an hour to search the visible and invisible Web.)

d. When the search is complete, click OK and click the Score button to arrange the search results according to how closely they match your query statement. (If the search has been interrupted, you may need to click Score twice to list the best results first.)

e. Click the Show Advanced Tools button beneath the Results Window, if necessary.

f. Click the top page in your Results Window, click the View as Text button and scroll down the Local Text Viewer window to examine the search-related terms highlighted in blue.

g. You decide that this page contains the kind of search terms you want. To find similar pages in your results, close the Local Text Viewer, and with the top page still highlighted click the Mark button and then click the Re-rank button above the Results Window. LexiBot ranks the pages based on how closely they match the search terms on the marked page.

h. Click the Rank button at the top of the column in the Results Window twice to rearrange the pages from closest to least likely match.

i. Use the Local Text Viewer to examine several of the pages at the top of the results list.

j. To share the results of this search with a friend, click File on the menu bar, click the Export Results command, and then click the Displayed Results as a Web Page command. When the Save HTML Export File As dialog box opens, type **invisible Web** in the File name text box, and then use the Save in textbox to select a drive and/or folder to store the Web page. Click the Save button.

k. Your browser opens with the results displayed in a Web page. Print the Web page and add your name to the top of the printout.

l. Click File on the menu bar on LexiBot, click the Exit command, and then OK in the File Not Saved dialog box to close the program.

► Visual Workshop

Knowing of your interest in hybrid cars, a friend gave you the following posting from a Usenet newsgroup. Try to locate the original thread. (*Hint:* Use the Advanced Search at Google's Groups Search engine). Once you locate the thread, print the posting and put your name at the top of the printout.

FIGURE D-20

Messages 1-10 from thread

Next 4

Jump to [End of thread]

From: Will Stewart (v_stewartSP@AMGOearthlink.net)   Message 1 in thread
Subject: Hybrid car sales are humming
Newsgroups: sci.environment, sci.energy, rec.autos.driving
Date: 2001-11-27 02:39:58 PST   View this article only

```
Jym Dyer wrote:

> >> It's entirely possible that, overall, it's more
> >> environmentally friendly to keep an old car going than
> >> to replace it every few years.

One can sell an old car to someone who will keep it going.

> =v= There's a lot of energy and pollution that go into building
> any new car.  One estimate is that 50% of the air pollution
> that comes from a car occurs during its manufacture.  There's
> no reason to believe that the manufacture of hybrid cars and
> EVs are going to be any different.
```

Project Files List
Read the following information carefully!!

---

1. Find out from your instructor the location of the Project Files you need and the location where you will store your files.

- To complete the units in this book, you need to use Project Files. Your instructor will either provide you with a copy of the Project Files or ask you to make your own copy.

- If you need to make a copy of the Project Files, you will need to copy a set of files from a file server, standalone computer, or the Web to the drive and location where you will be storing your Project Files.

- Your instructor will tell you which computer, drive letter, and folders contain the files you need, and where you will store your files.

- You can also download the files by going to www.course.com. See the inside back cover of the book for instructions to download your files.

---

2. Copy and organize your Project Files.

Floppy disk users

- If you are using floppy disks to store your Project Files, this list shows which files you'll need to copy onto your disk(s).

- Unless noted in the Project Files list, you will need one formatted, high-density disk for each unit. For each unit you are assigned, copy the files listed in the **Project File Supplied column** onto one disk.

- Make sure you label each disk clearly with the unit name (e.g., Internet Research Unit A).

- When working through the unit, save all your files to this disk.

Users storing files in other locations

- If you are using a zip drive, network folder, hard drive, or other storage device, use the Project Files List to organize your files.

- Create a subfolder for each unit in the location where you are storing your files, and name it according to the unit title (e.g., Internet Research Unit A).

- For each unit you are assigned, copy the files listed in the **Project File Supplied column** into that unit's folder.

- Store the files you modify or create in each unit in the unit folder.

---

3. Find and keep track of your Project Files and completed files.

- Use the **Project File Supplied column** to make sure you have the files you need before starting the unit or exercise indicated in the **Unit and Location column**.

- Use the **Student Saves File As column** to find out the filename you use when saving your changes to a Project File provided.

- Use the **Student Creates File column** to find out the filename you use when saving your new file for the exercise.

Unit and Location	Project File Supplied	Student Saves File As	Student Creates File
Unit A			
Lessons	IR-A1.rtf	Searching the Internet.rtf	
Skills Review	SR-A.rtf	IR Skills Review-A.rtf	
Independent Challenge 1			Unit A IC1.rtf
Independent Challenge 2			Unit A IC2.rtf
Independent Challenge 4			Unit A IC4.rtf
Visual Workshop			Unit A VW.rtf
Unit B			
Lessons	IR-B1.rtf	Deep Searches.rtf	
Skills Review	SR-B.rtf	IR Skills Review-B.rtf	
Unit C			
Lessons	IR-C1.rtf	Subject Guides.rtf	
Skills Review	SR-C.rtf	IR Skills Review-C.rtf	
Independent Challenge 1			Unit C IC1.rtf
Independent Challenge 2			Unit C IC2.rtf
Independent Challenge 3			Unit C IC3.rtf
Independent Challenge 4			Unit C IC4.rtf
Unit D			
Lessons	IR-D1.rtf	Specialty Information.rtf	
Skills Review	SR-D.rtf	IR Skills Review-D.rtf	

Glossary

Algorithm   A mathematical formula that a search engine uses to rank each Web site according to the terms used in your search query.

AND   A Boolean operator that connects the keywords you use in your search. Each time you add another AND to your search, you are further narrowing the search because the words on either side of AND must *both* be on a Web page for that Web page to be included in your search results. Many search engines use AND as the default Boolean operator, whether you enter it or not. See also *Boolean operator*.

AND NOT   A Boolean operator that narrows your search so that you find fewer pages than if you hadn't used it. If you use AND NOT in your search, the keyword or phrase that follows AND NOT will **not** appear on any of the Web pages returned by the search. See also *Boolean operator*.

Annotation   A carefully written summary or review. Subject guides generally include annotations of the Web sites listed.

Bookmarks   A function of the Netscape browser that allows for easy storage, organization, and revisiting of Web pages. Called Favorites in Internet Explorer.

Boolean logic   The field of mathematics that defines how Boolean operators manipulate large sets of data. Named after George Boole, it is also known as Boolean algebra.

Boolean operators   Command words such as AND, OR, and AND NOT that narrow, expand, or restrict a search based on Boolean logic.

Cached page   A copy of a Web page that resides on a search engine's computer.

Citation format   A style guide that standardizes references to resources like books, magazine articles, and Web pages. Common formats are MLA and APA.

Complex query   A search query that uses special connecting words and symbols called Boolean operators to define the relationships between keywords and phrases.

Corporate author   A committee, association, or group credited with creating a work such as a Web page.

Deep Web   See *invisible Web*.

Default operator   The Boolean term that a search engine automatically uses in a query whether the term is typed in the search text box or not. Most search engines default to the AND operator, although a few default to the OR operator.

Dewey Decimal system   A classification system used in many libraries. Named after its inventor Melville Dewey.

Directory   See *subject guide*.

Distributed subject guide   A Web site created by a variety of editors working somewhat independently. Like a regular subject guide, it hierarchically arranges links to Web pages based on topics and sub-topics. Though many distributed subject guides are excellent, they often lack standardization and can be uneven in quality. See also *subject guide*.

Dynamically generated Web pages   Pages that a database generates based on a specific database query. An example of the kinds of pages found in the invisible Web.

Evaluative criteria   Standards you use to determine if a Web site is right for your needs.

Favorites   A function of the Internet Explorer browser that allows for easy storage, organization, and revisiting of Web pages. Called Bookmarks in Netscape.

Filter   See *search filter*.

Forcing the order of operation   Using parentheses in a complex query that commands the search engine to look at the words inside the parentheses first.

GIF   An image file format often found on the Web.

Hierarchy   A ranked order. Hierarchies commonly used in Internet subject guides are topical and alphabetical.

HTML Hypertext markup language. See also *Web page*.

Intelligent search agent A software program that automates search activities, such as metasearching and database access. It aids in access to the invisible Web. Also called a search bot. One example is LexiBot.

Internet An enormous network of networks that share a common communication standard. It enables computers all over the world to exchange information.

Intersection The place where two sets overlap.

Invisible Web The part of the Web hidden from search engine spiders. It consists of information housed in databases, as well as much of the data in .pdf and .doc files. Also known as the deep Web.

JPG An image file format often found on the Web. Also called JPEG.

Keyword An important word from your research topic used to construct a search query.

List address The mailing list address where correspondence is sent. See also *subscription address*.

Listserv A software program that supports interactive Internet communication, such as the use of mailing lists.

Mailing list One form of interactive Internet communication. Often called a Listserv after the software that supports it.

Metasearch engine A search engine that searches multiple search engines.

Mnemonic Assisting or aiding memory. For example, many URLs are mnemonic to make it easier for users to remember them.

Morphing Finding variant spellings and forms of words. Used to prepare keywords for inclusion in a search query.

MOV A video file format often found on the Web.

MP3 An audio file format often found on the Web.

NEAR/ A Boolean operator that lets you perform a search while limiting the distance between specific keywords on a Web page. See also *Proximity operator*.

Netiquette The protocol and common rules of courtesy used by people on the Internet.

Newsgroup A form of interactive Internet communication. It is a virtual bulletin board where messages on thousands of topics are posted daily. Often called a Usenet newsgroup after the software upon which it runs.

OR Whenever you connect keywords in your search with the Boolean operator OR, you are commanding the search engine to find *either* of the keywords on a Web page. Therefore, each time you add another OR to your search you are expanding the search to include more Web pages. See also *Boolean operator*.

Order of operation See *Forcing the order of operation*.

Periodical database A specialized database that contains the full text of newspaper and magazine articles. Common periodical databases available at libraries are ProQuest, InfoTrac, and EbscoHost. This kind of database usually requires a paid subscription.

Phrase searching Looking for two or more words together, one right after the other. The most restrictive form of proximity searching, it is commonly achieved at an Internet search engine by putting quotation marks around the phrase.

Portal A large Web gateway that gives access to huge amounts of information. It often includes search engines, news, shopping, e-mail, chat, and more. A portal that focuses on one topic or industry is called a vertical portal, or vortal.

Proximity operator A Boolean command that tells a search engine how close keywords should be to each other on a Web page. Examples are W/ (within), NEAR/, and phrase searching using quotation marks.

Query See *search query*.

Scope The range of topics covered by a Web site.

Search bot See *Intelligent search agent*.

Search engine A search tool that helps you locate information on the Internet.

Search filter A program that a search engine uses to screen out Web pages and other files on the World Wide Web. Search filters are usually located at a search engine's Advanced Search page.

Search form A place where a user enters a search query at a search engine. It can be as simple as one text box, or a complex array of text boxes, filters, and pull-down menus.

Search query The keywords, phrases, and Boolean operators a user enters into a search text box.

Set The term used for a group in Boolean logic. In a Venn diagram a set is commonly represented as a circle.

Site map An index to the pages on a Web site.

Specialized research tool A program that gives you access to data stored in online databases that require direct access, making traditional search engines and most subject guides ineffective. Specialized research tools include online telephone directories, online maps, and online periodicals.

Specialized search engine A search engine that is limited by topic to the part of the Web it searches. A specialized search engine often combines the power of Boolean searching with the focus of a subject guide.

Spider A computer program that a search engine uses to travel from one Web site to another in order to index the contents of the Web pages. The spider-created index is what is searched when you query a search engine.

Stem A series of letters that a group of words have in common.

Subject directory See *Subject guide*.

Subject guide A Web site that hierarchically arranges links to Web pages. The links are chosen by people (often subject specialists or librarians) who evaluate and annotate the listings. Also called subject directory, subject index (or index), or subject tree.

Subject index See *Subject guide*.

Subject tree See *Subject guide*.

Subscription address A mailing list address where messages asking the administrator to add or drop a name from the list are sent. Also known as the administrative address. See also *list address*.

Synonyms Words that have similar meanings.

Thread A sub-topic of newsgroup postings.

Trailblazer page A Web page that links to sites that cover all aspects of a topic.

Truncating Cutting off the part of the word beyond the stem.

Union The combination of two sets.

Usenet See *newsgroup*.

Venn diagrams Drawings used to illustrate how Boolean operators work. First developed by John Venn.

Visible Web The portion of the Web that is indexed by search engine spiders.

Vortal A vertical portal. See also *portal*.

W/ A Boolean operator that will find the words you use as keywords in your argument within a specified number of words of each other, and only in the order you specify. See also *Proximity operator*.

Web See *World Wide Web*.

Web page The most common type of document on the World Wide Web. Web pages are usually written in hypertext markup language (HTML for short) and have file extensions of .htm or .html.

Web site Stores, links, and delivers Web pages. A Web site can range in size from one Web page to thousands of Web pages.

Wildcard A symbol that stands in for a single letter or a series of letters in a word. A common wildcard is the asterisk (*).

World Wide Web A vast collection of documents and other media linked together over the Internet. Also referred to as WWW, or the Web.

Index